userfirst GUIDES
services

MadCap Flare™
for RoboHelp™ users

Use your knowledge of RoboHelp to
get started fast with MadCap Flare!

by **Scott DeLoach**

MadCap Flare for RoboHelp Users
Scott DeLoach

Designer: Patrick Hofmann

Copy editor: Trina Dilbeck

Copyright © 2006 by Scott DeLoach

User First Services
11877 Douglas Rd
Suite 102-287
Alpharetta, GA 30005

www.userfirst.net

Notice of Rights
All rights reserved. No part of this book may be reproduced or transmitted in any form by any means, electronic, mechanical, photocopying, recording, or otherwise, without the prior written permission of the publisher. For information on obtaining permission for reprints and excerpts, contact permissions@userfirst.net.

Disclaimer
The information in this book is distributed on an "As Is" basis, without warranty. While every precaution has been taken in the preparation of this book, neither the author nor User First Services shall have any liability to any person or entity with respect to any loss or damage caused or alleged to be caused directly or indirectly by the instructions contained in this book or by the computer software described in it.

Trademarks
Trademarked names are used throughout this book. Rather than put a trademark symbol in every occurrence of a trademarked name, I state I am using the names only in an editorial fashion and to the benefit of the trademark owner with no intention of infringement of the trademark. All trademarks or service marks are the property of their respective owners.

ISBN: 978-1-4116-8747-9

9 8 7 6 5 4 3 2 1

Printed and bound in the United States of America

Dedication

This book is dedicated to my mother, Sylvia Jo DeLoach.
Thanks, mom, for always believing in me.

Contents

Introduction   9
Icons used in this book   9
Updates   9

Five reasons to use Flare   11
XML-based architecture and clean code   11
Multiple open topics and multiple undo   11
DotNet Help   11
Table stylesheets   12
Variables and snippets   12

Five reasons to use RoboHelp   13
Older browser support   13
Older Microsoft Word version support   13
Section 508 support   13
RoboHelp Pro's usage reports   13
WinHelp, JavaHelp, and Oracle help support   14

New features in Flare   15

RoboHelp features that are not in Flare...yet!   17
'What about FrameMaker and Acrobat files?'   19

Top ten Flare 'gotchas'   21
10 Viewing browse sequences   21
9   Opening multiple topics   21
8   Clicking condition tag boxes   21
7   Indexing   22
6   Auto-generating a TOC   22

5 Using templates	22
4 Using master pages	23
3 RoboHelp's WebHelp vs Flare's WebHelp	23
2 Finding the Code Editor	23
1 Importing HTML files	24

Comparing the RoboHelp and Flare GUIs   25

Projects   27

'What languages does Flare support?'	27
Creating a new project	28
Importing a project	30

'What happens to my... ?'   33

'Where is my dictionary?' TIP▶	34
'Where are my WebHelp skins?'	35
'Where are my kadov tags?'	35

Topics   37

'What is XHTML?'	37
'Do I have to know XML to use Flare?'	37
Creating a topic	37
Viewing your topic titles TIP▶	39
Opening a topic	40
Opening a topic in the Text Editor TIP▶	40
Opening a topic in another editor TIP▶	41
Opening two topics side by side NEW!	41
Using structure bars in a topic NEW!	42
Finding an open topic	43
Closing all open topics	43

Lists — 45
Creating a list — 46
Sorting a list NEW! — 46

Tables — 47
Creating a table — 47
Creating table styles NEW! — 50

Importing Word documents — 57
Creating a new project based on a Word document — 57
Importing a Word document — 60

Importing HTML, XHTML, and XML files — 63

Images and videos — 65
Inserting an image or video — 65
'How do I see which files use an image or video?' — 67

Links — 69
'Where's the link view?' — 69
Creating links — 69

Popup links — 75
'What about custom-sized popups?' — 75
Creating a topic popup link — 75
Creating a text popup link — 77

Drop-down, expanding, and toggler links — 79
'What is the difference?' — 79
Creating a drop-down link — 80
Creating an expanding link — 81
Creating a toggler link NEW! — 82

Related topics, keyword, and concept links — 85

'What is the difference?'	85
Creating a related topics link	86
Creating a keyword link	87
Creating a concept link	88

Browse sequences — 91

Creating a browse sequence	91
Creating a browse sequence based on your TOC [TIP]	95
Using a browse sequence	96
'Where are my HTML Help browse sequences?'	97

TOCs — 99

'Where's the TOC file?'	99
Making Flare look like RoboHelp: docking the TOC [TIP]	99
Manually creating a TOC	100
Auto-generating a TOC	102
Creating multiple TOCs [NEW]	104
Linking TOCs [NEW]	105
Associating a TOC with a target	106

Indexes — 107

'What about my RoboHelp index?'	107
Adding index entries using the 'quick term' method	108
Adding index entries using the Index Entry window method	108
Adding index entries using the Index Entry mode method [NEW]	110
Showing or hiding index entries in a topic	110
Viewing the index	111

Glossaries — 113

Creating a glossary	113
Making Flare look like RoboHelp: moving the glossary TIP	114
Adding terms to a glossary	115
Inserting glossary links for new terms	117
Using a glossary	118
'Where's the HTML Help glossary tab?'	119

Stylesheets — 121

Creating a stylesheet	122
Importing a stylesheet	123
Creating a style	124
Modifying a style	125
Creating a style medium	127
Associating a topic with a stylesheet	128
Associating multiple topics with a stylesheet	129

Master pages — 131

'Where's my RoboHelp template?'	131
Creating a master page	132
Adding a proxy to a master page NEW!	133
Associating a master page with a target	134

Skins — 135

'Where's the skin gallery?'	135
Creating a skin	135
Importing a skin	136
Editing a skin	137
Associating a skin with a target	138

Variables and snippets — 139

Variables	139
Importing a variable set	140
Creating a variable set	140
Snippets NEW!	145
Creating a snippet using existing content	145
Creating a snippet using new content	147
Inserting a snippet	148
Importing a snippet	149

Condition tags — 151

'What are those boxes in the Content Explorer?'	152
Importing condition tags	152
Creating a condition tag	153
Applying a tag to a topic, file, or folder	154
Applying a tag to content in a topic	155
Applying a tag to a TOC book or page NEW!	156
Applying a tag to an index entry NEW!	157

Targets — 159

'What is DotNet Help?' NEW!	159
'What about FlashHelp?'	160
'Is Flare's WebHelp the same as RoboHelp's WebHelp?'	160
Creating a target	162
Setting up a help target	163
Setting up a printed documentation target	165
Building a target	166
Building a target from the command line	167
Viewing a target	167
Publishing a target	168

Context-sensitive help — 171

Adding a header file	171
Creating an alias file	173
Testing context-sensitive help	175

Keyboard shortcuts (by task) — 177

Opening projects and topics	177
Selecting text	177
Formatting text	178
Linking	178
Saving	179
Spell checking	179
Working with the index and TOC	179
Searching	180
Opening and docking windows	180
Publishing	180
Opening Flare's help system	181

Keyboard shortcuts (by key) — 183

Toolbar comparison — 187

RoboHelp's Project toolbar	187
RoboHelp's Objects toolbar	188
RoboHelp's Formatting toolbar	189

Guide to Flare files — 191

'What about all those other RoboHelp files?'	192

Quick task index — 193

Projects	194
Topics	195
Topic content	196

Links	197
Drop-down, expanding, and toggler links	198
Related topic, keyword, and concept links	199
Navigational tools	200
Formatting	201
Variables and snippets	202
Condition tags	203
Targets	204
Context-sensitive help	205

Index　　　　　　　　　　　　　　　　　207

Introduction

This book was designed to help you get started quickly using MadCap Flare. It provides task and features comparisons between RoboHelp and Flare so you can leverage your existing knowledge of RoboHelp to learn Flare. If you are not a RoboHelp user, you can learn about RoboHelp and Flare at the same time!

Icons used in this book

The following icons are used throughout this book to help you find important and time-saving information.

Icon	Meaning	Description
⚠	Caution	Important advice that could cause data loss or unnecessary aggravation if not followed.
NEW!	New Feature	A feature in Flare v1.0 that is not in RoboHelp x5.
◇	Note	Additional information about a topic.
TIP▶	Tip	A recommended best practice, shortcut, or workaround.

Updates

For the most up-to-date information about this book, see www.userfirst.net.

For the most up-to-date information about Flare, see MadCap software's website at www.madcapsoftware.com.

Introduction | 9

Five reasons to use Flare

Flare is the most technologically-advanced help authoring tool available. In addition to its innovative user interface and excellent online help, Flare provides many key features that help authors have been requesting for years. This section lists five reasons that I use Flare and recommend it to clients.

XML-based architecture and clean code

Flare's XML-based architecture means that MadCap will be able to add support for DITA, DocBook, MAML, and other XML schemas in the future. All of Flare's project files are XML-based, so they're extremely small and easy to read.

Flare's XML-based authoring means that it produces clean code. No more kadov tags!

Multiple open topics and multiple undo

Unlike RoboHelp, Flare allows you to open multiple topics at the same time. You can even view two topics side by side.

Flare also provides undo and redo commands back to the last time you saved your project. Flare maintains separate undo and redo for each open topic, so you can undo actions you performed in one topic without undoing actions you performed in other open topics.

DotNet Help

DotNet Help is MadCap's new help format for .NET applications. It's also a great solution for server-based help, especially since Microsoft's recent security 'fixes' disable HTML Help from running on a server and block WebHelp's active content (in Internet Explorer) when it's run from a file server or locally.

Table stylesheets

In other help authoring tools and HTML editors, you must use inline formatting to format tables. Most users copy and paste a blank table to create a new table, but it's inefficient and hard to maintain consistency.

In Flare, you can use table stylesheets to format tables. You can create multiple table stylesheets that specify borders, background colors, captions, and other table style properties. You can even create headers, footers, and alternating row and column background colors.

Variables and snippets

Variables and snippets allow you to reuse content in topics. Variables are perfect for short text strings such as product names. If the product's name changes, you can change the variable and all of the inserted variable references are updated. Flare's system variables can be used to insert the time and date or, for printed documentation, the page number and page count.

Snippets can be used to insert any content, including text, images, and tables. You can use snippets to reuse a note, a procedure, or even a screenshot and its description.

Five reasons to use RoboHelp

RoboHelp and Flare are both great applications. I've used RoboHelp for over ten years, and I've been a certified RoboHelp instructor for the last seven. This section lists five reasons that I will continue to use RoboHelp for certain projects.

Older browser support

RoboHelp's WebHelp supports very old browsers. It may look very plain and some features may be disabled, but it *will* work. If you need to create WebHelp that will run in very old browsers such as Netscape Navigator 4.0, RoboHelp is the perfect application to use.

Older Microsoft Word version support

Flare requires Microsoft Word 2003. Many companies still use older versions of Word and do not allow individual departments to upgrade by themselves. If a client cannot upgrade to Word 2003, I recommend that they use RoboHelp until they can upgrade.

Section 508 support

RoboHelp's WebHelp provides limited Section 508 support in its navigational controls (the TOC, index, and search). Of course, it's up to you as the help author to make sure that your content is Section 508 compliant.

RoboHelp Pro's usage reports

With RoboHelp Pro, you can create usage reports to monitor how your users are using your online help or policies and procedures. Although the technology needs to be updated, RoboHelp Pro's reports are a great resource. You can use them to identify new topics, common questions, and errors in your help system. You can also use them to prove how often users use your information.

WinHelp, JavaHelp, and Oracle help support

I use RoboHelp for Word to maintain WinHelp (.hlp) help systems. It has always worked very well for me, and many legacy help projects do not need to move to a newer format or help authoring tool.

I recommend RoboHelp HTML to clients who are creating JavaHelp and Oracle Help help systems. If they can use WebHelp instead of JavaHelp or Oracle Help, I recommend comparing Flare's WebHelp to RoboHelp's WebHelp.

New features in Flare

Flare includes the following new features that are not found in RoboHelp:

Feature	Description	See page
Block and span bars	Flare displays your tags in block and span bars. You can select tags to move, sort, or modify content.	42
Command line compiling	You can build DotNet Help, HTML Help, WebHelp, or printed documentation directly from the command line. This feature allows programmers to build your help when they compile an application.	167
Conditional index and TOC entries	In Flare, you can apply a condition tag to anything, including index and TOC entries.	156
Configurable user interface	You can move windows wherever you want and save your window layout. You can even create multiple layouts for different tasks.	99
Cross references and hyperlinks in printed documentation	Cross references and hyperlinks are converted when you create printed documentation.	165
DotNet Help format	DotNet Help is MadCap's help format for .NET applications. Unlike HTML Help and WebHelp, it can also run from a file server.	159
Multiple TOCs	You can create and use multiple TOCs for different versions of a help system, for printed documentation, or even allow each help author to create and maintain a TOC for their topics.	104
Multiple open documents	Need to copy and paste content between topics? Just open them both—you can even open them side by side. In Flare you can open as many topics as you need.	41

Feature	Description	See page
Table stylesheets	Table stylesheets can be used to specify table borders, shading patterns, and padding.	50
Unicode support	Unicode allows you to write content in virtually any language without installing a specific-language version.	27
Variables and snippets	Need to reuse a short string of text, like a product name? Just create a variable! Need to reuse formatted content, such as a table? Just create a snippet!	139

RoboHelp features that are not in Flare...yet!

Yes, there are some features in RoboHelp that are not in Flare v1.0. Here's a list:

Feature	What You Should Do
Custom-sized popups	Use an auto-sized popup. Flare does a much better job of auto-sizing popups than RoboHelp, but you cannot create custom-sized popups. See 'What about custom-sized popups?' for more information.
FlashHelp	Use WebHelp. MadCap has announced that they will release a Flash-based help format, but they are waiting for a bug to be fixed in the Flash player. See 'What about FlashHelp?' for more information.
Forms	Use another HTML editor to create and edit forms. To open a topic in another HTML editor, right-click the topic and select **Open with** > *your HTML editor*.
FrameMaker import	Save the FrameMaker file as an HMTL file and import the HTML file. See 'What about FrameMaker and Acrobat files' for more information.
JavaHelp	Use DotNet Help or WebHelp. If you cannot use DotNet Help or WebHelp, contact MadCap Software and ask them to add support for JavaHelp. The MadCap team is very interested in user feedback. If they see enough interest, they may add support for JavaHelp.
Link View	Right-click a topic and select **Show Dependencies**. Flare does not have a graphical link view like RoboHelp, but it does provide a list of files that link to the selected topic.

Feature	What You Should Do
Oracle Help	Consider using DotNet Help or WebHelp. If you can't use either of these formats, ask MadCap to add support for Oracle Help. The MadCap team knows that they cannot create one tool that meets everyone needs. However, they may add an Oracle Help target type if enough users are interested.
PDF import	Save the PDF file as an HTML file and import the HTML file. See 'What about FrameMaker and Acrobat files' for more information.
Reports	**Broken Links:** Review the log file when you create a target.-If you save the log, it appears in the Reports folder in the Project Organizer. You can double click an error in the log to open the corresponding topic. **Images:** Right-click a topic and select **Show Dependencies**. Flare will display a list of topics that include the image. **Stylesheets:** Right-click the stylesheet and select **Show Dependencies**. Flare will display a list of topics that use the stylesheet. **TOC report:** Flare's TOC Editor automatically identifies TOC pages that are not linked to topics. **Topic References:** Right-click the topic and select **Show** Dependencies. Flare will display a list of topics that link to the current topic.
RoboSource Control	Use a source control program such as WinCVS or Microsoft Visual Source Safe.
RoboHelp's Tools	Use Flare's integrated features. Flare does not include RoboHelp's tools, the small applications that appear on the Tools tab. However, it does provide multi-file search and replace and publishing features.
What's This Help? Composer	Use Flare's Alias Editor to create context-sensitive DotNet Help, HTML Help, or WebHelp.

'What about FrameMaker and Acrobat files?'

MadCap Software has announced plans to add round-trip FrameMaker .fm file importing and exporting and Acrobat .pdf export to Flare v2.0. For details, see the MadCap website at www.madcapsoftware.com.

Top ten Flare 'gotchas'

RoboHelp and Flare are similar, but there are some features that are *just* different enough to be confusing at first. There are also a few Flare features that can be hard to find, especially if you are accustomed to using RoboHelp.

Here's my list of the top ten features that I had trouble understanding, finding, or remembering how to use when I started using Flare.

10 Viewing browse sequences

In RoboHelp, browse sequences appear as either a graphical bar at the top of your topics (HTML Help) or as small arrows in the navigation pane (WebHelp). RoboHelp's HTML Help browse sequences require the ActiveX.dll file to be installed on the user's computer.

In Flare, browse sequences appear as either a TOC item (HTML Help) or as an accordion item (WebHelp). Because they do not appear on a custom tab, Flare's HTML Help browse sequences do not require a .dll file.

9 Opening multiple topics

In RoboHelp, you can only have one topic open at a time. In Flare, you can have multiple topics open at the same time. The only downside is that you may be used to RoboHelp closing a topic when you open a new topic. When I started using Flare, I often had 15 or 20 topics open before I realized it. Fortunately, Flare provides a 'Close all' menu command.

8 Clicking condition tag boxes

Flare's Content Explorer uses condition tag boxes to identify topics that use condition tags. Unfortunately, an empty condition tag box looks like a checkbox. I tried to select these boxes for a few days and thought they must be broken. According to the Flare help community, many other users assume they are checkboxes too.

7 Indexing

Indexing is very different in Flare than in RoboHelp. Although Flare does not include an indexing wizard, it does include an 'Index Entry Mode' especially for indexers to add keyword terms. Flare also supports conditional index entries.

6 Auto-generating a TOC

In RoboHelp, you can auto-generate a TOC based on your Project tab. Folders on the Project tab become books, and topics become pages. If you change the organization on the Project tab, you have to regenerate the TOC or update it yourself.

In Flare, you can auto-generate a TOC book to automatically create links to headings inside a topic. If you add or remove headings in the topic, the TOC is automatically updated.

5 Using templates

In RoboHelp, a template is used to format topics and include boilerplate content, such as a logo or a header and footer. The headers and footers are dynamically linked to topics. If you change a template's header or footer, topics that use the template are automatically updated.

In Flare, everything (including stylesheets, snippets, tables, topics, and TOCs), uses a template. You can use a template to include boilerplate content and formatting, but it is not dynamically linked to the item you created. If you update a template, the items that used that template are not updated. However, Flare's master pages *do* allow you to dynamically update topics.

4 Using master pages

Flare's master pages are similar to RoboHelp's templates, but they provide more features. You can use a master page to add breadcrumb paths and mini-toc links to your online help. Or, you can use a master page to include headings, footers, chapter names, page numbers, or the total page count in your printed documentation.

3 RoboHelp's WebHelp vs Flare's WebHelp

RoboHelp's WebHelp is not the same as Flare's WebHelp. Here are a few key differences:

Feature	RoboHelp	Flare
Browse sequences	The topic list and other browse sequence groups are not visible.	The topic list and browse sequence groups are visible, similar to a TOC.
Browser support	Supports very old browsers: ▫ IE 5.0 and later ▫ Netscape 4.0 and later	Requires a more recent browser: ▫ IE 5.5 and later ▫ Netscape 6.0 and later
Default navigational controls	Tabs	Accordion items
Search highlighting		✓
Search filtering		✓
Section 508 support	✓	

2 Finding the Code Editor

Unlike RoboHelp, Flare makes it a little tricky to find the Code Editor. You can open a 'pseudo code' editor using a toolbar button, but you need to right-click a topic and select **Open with** > **Internal Editor** to open a topic in the Code Editor.

Top ten Flare 'Gotchas' | 23

1 Importing HTML files

Flare does not include an 'Import HTML File' command. Instead, any HTML files that are stored in your Content folder appear in your project. To import an HTML file, just copy it to your Content folder. It will be converted to XHTML when you open it in Flare.

TIP *If you add a folder containing HTML files to the Content folder, the folder and all of the HTML files appear in your project.*

Comparing the RoboHelp and Flare GUIs

RoboHelp and Flare have similar GUIs ('graphical user interfaces'), but they often use slightly different terms for similar features. The following table matches RoboHelp's interface elements with their Flare equivalents.

RoboHelp	Flare
Project tab	Project Organizer and Content Explorer
TOC tab	TOC Editor
Index tab	Index Entry window and Index Explorer
Glossary tab	Glossary Editor
Tools tab	N/A, but Flare does include a multi-file spell-checking tool, a broken links log, and a file dependencies list.
WYSIWYG Editor	XML Editor
TrueCode Editor	Internal Text Editor
Link View	N/A, but the Link Dependencies window provides a list.
Topics List	N/A

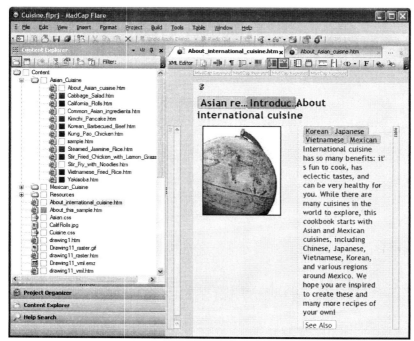

Flare user interface

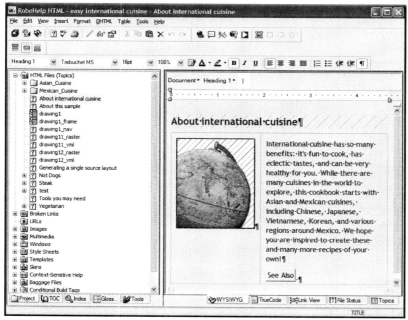

RoboHelp user interface

26 | Comparing the RoboHelp and Flare GUIs

Projects

In RoboHelp, project files have either a .xpj (X5) or .mpj (X4 and earlier) extension. In Flare, project files have a .flprj extension (for 'Flare project'). Flare's project file is a small XML file—feel free to open it in Notepad and take a look.

The project file is stored in your project's top-level folder. You name this folder when you create a new project. For example, if your project is named 'MyFirstProject,' your top-level folder is named 'MyFirstProject.' By default, Flare creates your top-level folder in the My Documents\My Projects folder.

In addition to the project file, your top-level folder contains three subfolders: Content, Project, and Output.

The **Content** folder contains all of your topics, images, sounds, stylesheets, and videos.

The **Project** folder contains your conditional tag sets, context-sensitive help map files, glossaries, skins, TOCs, and variable sets. Wondering where the index file is? There's not one—Flare stores your keywords in your topics.

The **Output** folder contains your generated targets, like HTML Help or printed documentation. It's similar to RoboHelp's !SSL! folder.

'What languages does Flare support?'

Although it may support many other languages, MadCap has only tested and officially announced support for the following languages:

- Danish
- Dutch
- English
- Finnish
- French
- German
- Italian
- Norwegian
- Portuguese
- Portuguese (Brazilian)
- Spanish
- Swedish

MadCap has announced plans to support many more languages in the future, including double-byte languages such as Chinese and Japanese. Some users have already used Flare v1.0 successfully with Russian, Chinese, and Japanese.

Creating a new project

Creating a project in Flare is very similar to creating a project in RoboHelp. In both applications, you begin by naming the project and selecting a folder, target, and language.

You can create a new project using a project template. In fact, you can use a template when you create anything in Flare, such as topics, stylesheets, glossaries, skins, and variables. Templates allow you to include content or formatting when you create a new item. For example, Flare includes a project template named 'Application Help Sample.' If you create a project using this template, Flare will create some sample topics for you: 'Contacting,' Getting Started,' 'Introduction,' 'Welcome,' and What's New.' If you want to create a blank project, you can use the 'Empty' template.

Shortcut	Toolbar	Menu
Ctrl+O		File > New Project

To create a new project:

1. Click in the toolbar.
   —OR—
   Select **File** > **New Project**.
   —OR—
   Press **Ctrl+O**.

The Start New Project wizard appears.

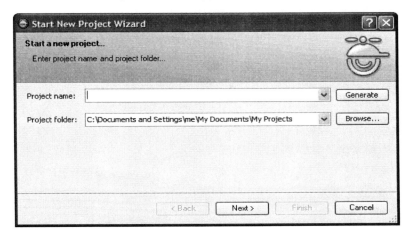

2   Type a **Project Name**.
    You don't have to type the .flprj extension. Flare will add it for you if you leave it out.

3   Type or select a **Project Folder** and click **Next**.

4   Select a **Language** and click **Next**.
    The language you select determines which dictionary is used for spell checking.

5   Select a **Template Folder**, select a **Template**, and click **Next**.

6   Select an **Available Target** and click **Next**.

7   Select **Create the Project**.

8   Click **Finish**.
    Your new project opens in Flare.

Importing a project

You can import projects created with RoboHelp X5 (xpj files), RoboHelp X4 and earlier (.mpj files), or other help authoring tools (.hhp files).

Shortcut	Toolbar	Menu
none	none	File > Import Project

To import a RoboHelp project:

1 Select **File** > **Import Project** > **Import (Non-Flare) Project**.
   The Import Project Wizard appears.

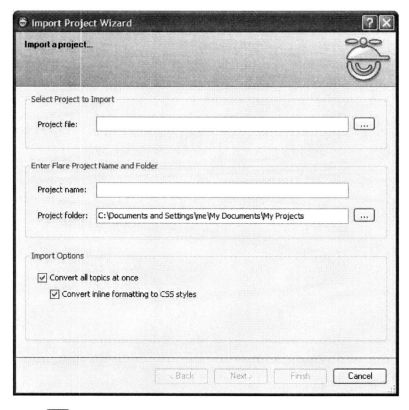

2 Click [...] to find a project file to import.
   The Open dialog box appears.

3. Locate and select a project file.
   - RoboHelp X5: .xpj file
   - RoboHelp X4 and earlier: .mpj file
   - Other tools: .hhp file
4. Click **Open**.
5. Type a **Project Name**.
6. Type or select a **Project Folder**.
7. Select whether you want to **Convert all topics at once**.
   This option converts your topic files from HTML to XHTML. If you do not select this option, your files will remain as HTML files with RoboHelp's non-standard tagging and your index terms will not be imported.
8. Select whether you want to **Convert inline formatting to CSS styles**.
   If your project used inline formatting, you should convert the inline formatting to styles. Styles are much easier to create and maintain.
9. Click **Finish**.
   The RoboHelp project is imported into Flare. Your new Flare project file will have a .flprj extension.

'What happens to my... ?'

The following table explains how RoboHelp's features convert to Flare.

RoboHelp Feature	Converts?	Comments
Browse Sequences	✓	
Conditional Tags	✓	Stored in a condition tag set named 'Primary.'
Custom colors		You must recreate the colors in Flare.
Dictionaries?		See 'Where's my dictionary?'
HTML Topics	✓	Converted to XHTML either when imported (recommended) or when opened.
Folders	✓	
Forms	✓	Forms are converted, but you cannot edit or create forms in Flare. To edit a form, right-click its topic and select **Open with** > *your HTML editor*.
Frames	✓	Frames are converted, but you cannot edit or create forms in Flare. To edit a frame, right-click its topic and select **Open with** > *your HTML editor*.
Glossary	✓	Stored in a glossary named 'Primary.'
Inline Formatting	✓	Maintained, or can be converted to styles.
Publishing Locations	✓	Converted to 'Publishing destinations.'
Single-Source Layouts.	✓	Converted to 'Targets'
Sounds	✓	
Table of Contents	✓	Converted to a TOC named 'Primary.'

RoboHelp Feature	Converts?	Comments
Template Headers and Footers	✓	Converted to snippets.
Videos	✓	
WebHelp Skins		See 'Where are my WebHelp skins?'
Windows	✓	Converted to skins.

'Where is my dictionary?' 💡

RoboHelp dictionaries are not imported, but you *can* move your dictionary terms to Flare.

To use your dictionary terms in Flare:

1   Close Flare.

2   In Windows Explorer, open the C:\Program Files\MadCap Software\MadCap Flare\Flare.app\Resources\SSCE folder.

3   Find your dictionary.
    Dictionary file names are based on their language. For example, Flare's 'English - American' dictionary is named 'ssceam.tlx.'

4   Just to be safe, make a backup copy of your dictionary.

5   Locate your RoboHelp dictionary.
    To find your dictionary:

    ▫ Open RoboHelp HTML.

    ▫ Select Tools > Spelling Options.

    ▫ Select the Dictionary tab. Your dictionaries' paths are listed in the Path column.

6   Open your RoboHelp dictionary in Notepad.

7   Copy all of your terms and close your RoboHelp dictionary.

8   Open your Flare dictionary in Notepad.

9   Paste your terms at the end of the file.

10 Save your new Flare dictionary.

'Where are my WebHelp skins?'

Unfortunately, RoboHelp skins are not imported into Flare. You will have to recreate them in Flare. You can use Flare's Skin Editor to fully customize your DotNet Help, HTML Help, and WebHelp targets.

'Where are my kadov tags?'

Flare doesn't need them, so it takes them out (thanks, MadCap!). RoboHelp is notorious for the 'kadov' tags it uses in stylesheets. If you're wondering what a kadov tag is, the commonly-told story is as follows:

> When RoboHelp was being developed, the programmer (yep, just one!) would work all day and all night coding. He started to get a little stir crazy from working so hard, so he created a game to stay sane. Whenever he ran into a problem that was either too time consuming or difficult to fix correctly, he used a special tag to force it to work. In exchange, he had to drink a shot. Many RoboHelp users who know the story think he must have been hammered when he finished!
>
> Eventually, the programmer finished his work and turned it in to Blue Sky Software Corporation, eHelp's name way back then. They thought everything looked great—until they noticed all of the special tags. They told him there was no way they could release a product with 'vodka' tags in it! It was too late to take them out, so they changed them to 'kadov' and a legend was born.

I'm not positive the story is true, but I've had it verified by many people who were in a position to know. I *do* know that there's a town named 'Kadov' in the Czech Republic. If you ever visit Kadov, send me a postcard!

Topics

One big difference between RoboHelp and Flare is that RoboHelp topics are HTML files and Flare topics are XHTML files.

'What is XHTML?'

According to the W3C, XHTML is the successor to HTML. XHTML files use HTML tags, but they conform to the much stricter rules of XML. For example, HTML does not require end tags for the <br>, <li>, or <img> tags. In XHTML, all tags must have end tags. So, a break is written in XHTML as <br />. Another difference is that HTML allows upper, lower, or mixed case tags: <BR>, <br>, or <Br>. In XHTML, you must use all lowercase.

'Do I have to know XML to use Flare?'

Like RoboHelp, Flare has a built-in WYSIWYG ('what-you-see-is-what-you-get') editor. In Flare, it's called the 'XML Editor.' You don't have to know anything about HTML, XHTML, or XML to use the XML Editor. Flare will do all of the tagging for you. If you *do* know how to tag content, you can view the code and change it yourself.

Creating a topic

Creating a topic in Flare is very similar to creating a topic in RoboHelp. One small difference with Flare is that all topics use a template. In RoboHelp, using a template is optional.

Shortcut	Toolbar	Menu
Ctrl+T	(Content Explorer toolbar)	Project > Add Topic

To create a topic:

1 Click ![icon] in the Content Explorer toolbar.
   —OR—
   Select **Project** > **Add Topic**.
   —OR—
   Press **Ctrl+T**.
   The Add New Topic dialog appears.

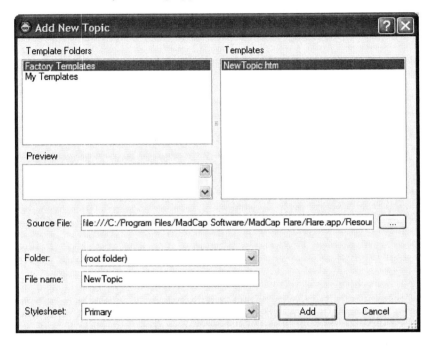

2 Select a **Template Folder** and **Template**.
   The template file that you select will appear as the **Source file**.

3 Select a **Folder** to contain the new topic.

4 Type a **File name** for the topic.
   You don't have to type the .htm extension. Flare will add it for you if you leave it out.

5 Select a **Stylesheet** to associate with the new topic.

6 Click **Add**.
   The Copy to Project dialog box appears.

7 Click **OK**.

The topic appears in the Content Explorer and opens in the XML Editor.

Viewing your topic titles 💡

In RoboHelp, most users view their topics by the topic titles. In Flare you can only view topics by their file name, unless you know how to find the topic titles! Flare hides them in the Details pane of the Content Explorer.

To view your topic titles:

1 Open the Content Explorer.

2 Click ⬚ in the Content Explorer toolbar.
The Details pane appears on the right side of the Content Explorer.

3 Scroll the **Details** pane to the **Title** column.

4 Click the **Title** column's heading and drag it to be the first column in the Details pane.

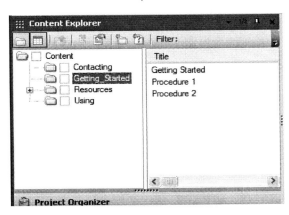

5 To open a folder, click a folder name in the left pane.
To open a topic, double-click its title in the right pane.

Topics | 39

Opening a topic

In Flare, your topics appear in the Content Explorer. When you double-click a topic, it opens as a new tab in the XML Editor.

Shortcut	Toolbar	Menu
Enter	(Content Explorer toolbar)	none

To open a topic:

1 Select a topic in the Content Explorer.

2 Press **Enter**.
   —OR—
   Click in the Content Explorer toolbar.
   The topic appears as a new tab in the XML Editor.

Opening a topic in the Text Editor

Flare's Text Editor is similar to RoboHelp's True Code editor. You can open a topic in the Text Editor to view and edit the HTML tags.

To open a topic in the Text Editor:

1 Open the Content Explorer.

2 Right-click a topic and select **Open With** > **Internal Text Editor**.
   The topic opens as a new tab in the Text Editor.

Opening a topic in another editor 💡▶

Like RoboHelp, Flare lets you open topics in other HTML editors—if you know where to look!

To open a topic in another HTML editor:

1 Open the Content Explorer.

2 Right-click a topic and select **Open With** > *your HTML editor*.
   The topic opens in the HTML editor you selected.

Opening two topics side by side 🆕

Unlike RoboHelp, Flare lets you open multiple topics at the same time. You can even open two topics side by side to compare or copy and paste content.

To open two topics side by side:

1 Open a topic.
   The topic opens as a new tab in the XML Editor.

2 Open another topic.
   The second topic opens as a new tab in the XML Editor.

3 Select **Window** > **Floating**.
   The selected topic appears in a small floating window.

Topics | 41

4   Click the floating window's title bar and drag the window.
    The positioning arrow appears.

5   Drag the window on top of one of the arrows.
    The target window location will be shaded light blue.

6   Release your mouse button.

📖 *To change the window back to 'normal,' select* **Window** > **Floating** *and drag the window to the center of the positioning arrow.*

Using structure bars in a topic NEW!

In Flare, you can use structure bars to view the tagging behind your topics. There are four structure bars: block, span, table column, and table row. The block and table row bars appear on the left side of the XML Editor, and the span and table column bars appear on the top.

Icon	Description
	Show/hide block bars
	Show/hide span bars
	Show/hide table row bars
	Show/hide table column bars

42 | Topics

Finding an open topic

If Flare does not have enough room to display each topic's tab, the additional topics appear in a drop-down list.

To find an open topic in the XML Editor:

1   Click the down arrow on the right side of the XML Editor.

2   Select a topic in the drop-down list.

Closing all open topics

In RoboHelp, you don't have to close a topic—just open a new topic and the previous topic closes. It's a small advantage to only having one topic open at a time!

When you start using Flare, you will probably forget to close topics. If you have too many topics open, you can close all of them at once.

To close all open windows:

▫   Select **Window** > **Close All Documents**.
    All of the open windows close.

Lists

Flare provides one toolbar button for both bulleted and numbered lists, so the icon on the button represents the last type of list you created. For example, if you add a bulleted list, the icon changes to a bulleted list.

You can create the following types of lists:

Type	Example
Bulleted list	▪
Circle bulleted list	○
Square bulleted list	▪
Numbered list	1, 2, 3
Lower-alpha numbered list	a, b, c
Upper-alpha numbered list	A, B, C
Lower-roman numbered list	i, ii, iii
Upper-roman numbered list	I, II, III

The bulleted list button is on the Text Format toolbar.

To view the Text Format toolbar:

- Click **F** in the XML Editor toolbar.
  —OR—
  Select **View** > **Toolbars** > **Text Formatting**.

Creating a list

You can select the list type when you create the list.

Shortcut	Toolbar	Menu
none	Text Format toolbar	none

To create a bulleted or numbered list:

1 Open a topic.

2 Position your cursor where you want to create the list.
   —OR—
   Highlight content that you want to format as a list.

3 Click the icon's down arrow.

   ◁ *The Lists icon may be a numbered or bulleted list.*

4 Select a list type.

5 If you are creating a new list, type the list items.

Sorting a list NEW!

Ever tried to sort a list in RoboHelp? Unfortunately, you can't. But you *can* sort a list in Flare.

To sort a list:

1 Select the list.

2 If you are not viewing tag block bars, click in the XML Editor toolbar.

3 Click the **ol** (numbered list) or **ul** (bulleted list) tag.

4 Select **Sort List** to sort the list.
   —OR—
   Select **Reverse List** to sort the list in reverse order.

Tables

In RoboHelp, you can create tables based on "formats," such as a dark blue background for the first row and a bright blue left background for the first column. RoboHelp uses inline formatting to format the table, so you have to manually update the table's formatting if you want to change it.

In Flare, you can create tables based on table styles. If you need to change the formatting, you can change the table style to update all of your tables. Flare also makes it easy to move, add, and delete table columns and rows.

Creating a table

Shortcut	Toolbar	Menu
none	none	Table > Insert > Table

To create a table:

1 Open a topic.

2 Position the cursor where you want to create the table.

3 Select **Table** > **Insert** > **Table**.

The Insert Table dialog box appears.

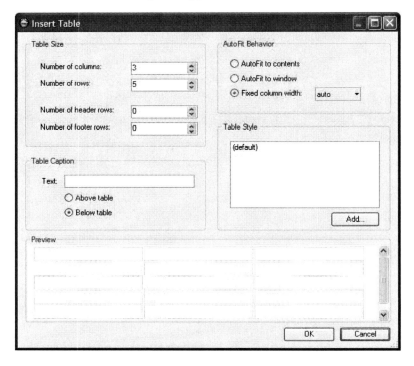

4   Type or select a **Number of Columns**.

5   Type or select a **Number of Rows**.

6   If needed, type or select a number of header and/or footer rows.

7   If needed, type a table caption and select a caption location.

8   Select a column width.

- **AutoFit to Contents** — each column's width is based on the amount of content it contains.

- **AutoFit to Window** — the columns are equally-sized to fit the size of the window.

- **Fixed Column Width** — each column is set to a specified width.

9   Click **OK**.

To add borders to a table:

1 Click inside a table.

2 Select **Table** > **Table Properties**.
The Table Properties dialog box appears.

3 Select the **Borders** tab.

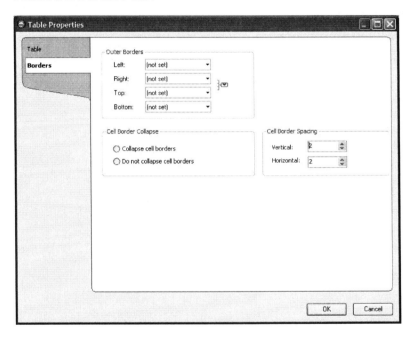

4 To add an **Outer Border**:
- Click the border's down arrow.
- Select a length.
- Select a color.
- Select a measurement amount and unit.
- Select a border style.
- Click OK.

5 Click **OK**.

Creating table styles NEW!

In Flare, you can create table styles to format your tables. For example, you can create a table style named "noBorders" to create tables without borders and another named "greenHeading" to create tables with a green background for headings.

Table styles are stored in table stylesheets.

Shortcut	Toolbar	Menu
none	none	Project > Add Table Style

To create a table styleheet:

1 Select **Project** > **Add Table Style**.
   The Add New Table Style dialog box appears.

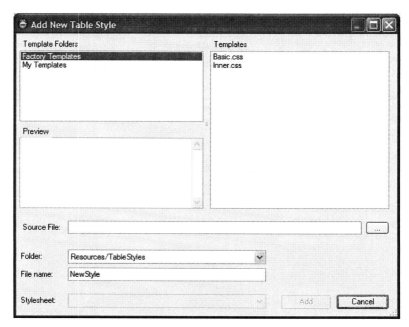

2 Select a **Template Folder** and **Template**.

50 | Tables

3 Select a **Folder**.
By default, table stylesheets are stored in the Resources\TableStyles folder.

4 Type a **File Name** for the table stylesheet.
Table stylesheets have a .css extension. If you don't type the extension, Flare will add it for you.

5 Click **Add**.
The Copy to Project dialog box appears.

6 Click **OK**.
The table stylesheet appears in the Content Explorer and opens in the TableStyle Editor.

To modify a table style:

1 Open a table stylesheet.
The TableStyle Editor appears.

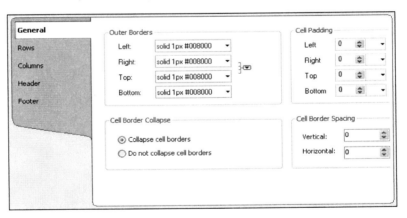

2 On the General tab, select the following options:

- **Outer Borders** — select the style, width, and color of your table borders.

- **Cell Padding** — select the amount of space between a cell's border and its content.

Tables | 51

- **Cell Border Collapse** — cell borders normally appear inside row borders. If you collapse them, they are merged with the row border.
- **Cell Border Spacing** — select the amount of space between cells.

3 Select the **Rows** tab.

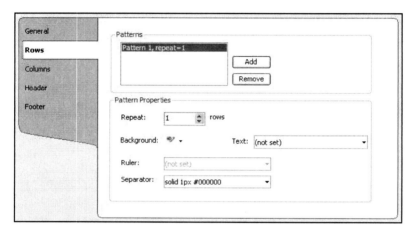

4 On the Rows tab, select the following options:
- **Patterns** — patterns can be used to provide different row formats, such as alternating background colors.
- **Pattern Properties** — if you use a pattern, select how many times the pattern should repeat, its background color, text color, and a separator border.

5 Select the **Columns** tab.

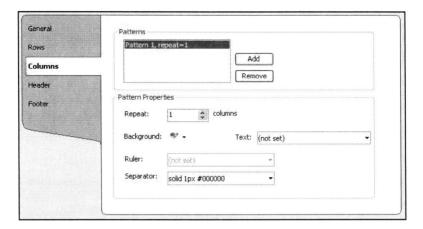

6 On the Columns tab, select the following options:

- **Patterns**— patterns can be used to provide different column formats, such as alternating background colors.

- **Pattern Properties** — if you use a pattern, select how many times the pattern should repeat, its background color, text color, and a separator border.

7 Select the **Header** tab.

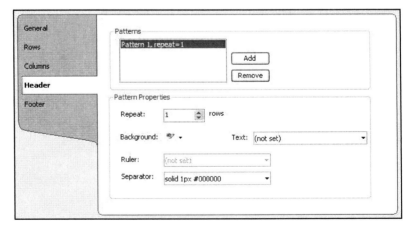

8 On the Header tab, select the following options:

- **Patterns** — patterns can be used to provide different header formats, such as a bottom border.

Tables | 53

- **Pattern Properties** — if you use a pattern, select how many times the pattern should repeat, its background color, text color, and a separator border.

9 Select the **Footer** tab.

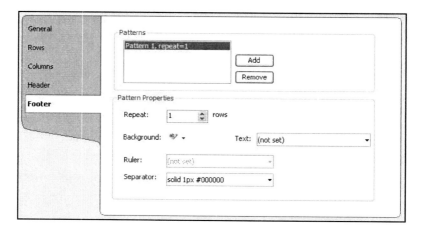

10 On the Footer tab, select the following options:

- **Patterns** — patterns can be used to provide different footer formats, such as a top border.
- **Pattern Properties** — if you use a pattern, select how many times the pattern should repeat, its background color, text color, and a separator border.

To assign a table stylesheet to a table:

1 Click inside the table.

2 Select **Table** > **Table Properties**.
The Table Properties dialog box appears.

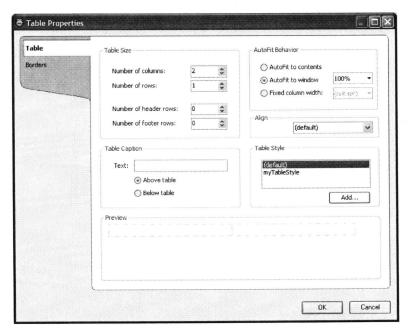

3 Select a **Table Style**.

4 Click **OK**.

Importing Word documents

Like RoboHelp, Flare allows you to import Word documents. When you import a Word document, you can convert your Word template to a stylesheet. You can even create multiple topics based on styles or length. For example, you can create a new topic every 10,000 characters. If you decide to split a long Word document into multiple topics, Flare can automatically add "continued from" and "continued in" links to your topics.

Creating a new project based on a Word document

You can create a new project based on a Word document in Flare and RoboHelp. The steps are very similar, but Flare includes some new features such as creating new topics based on length and automatically creating 'previous' and 'next' links.

Shortcut	Toolbar	Menu
none	none	File > Import Project > Import MS Word Documents

To create a new project based on a Word document:

1 Select **File** > **Import Project** > **Import MS Word Documents**.
The Import Microsoft Word wizard appears.

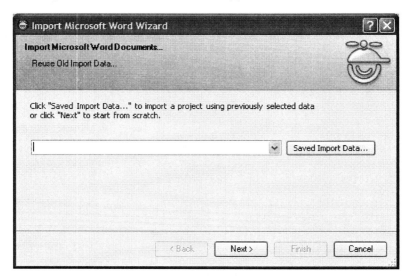

2 Click **Next**.
When you import a Word document, Flare saves your settings in an import data file (these files have a .flimp extension). You can reuse these settings when you re-import the Word document or import similar documents.

3 Click **Add Files**.

4 Select a file and click **Open**.
If needed, you can select more than one Word document.

5 If you plan to continue editing the file in Word, select **Link generated files to source files**.
This option links the imported topics to the Word document. When you re-import the document, Flare replaces the original topics with the new topics.

6 Click **Next**.

7 Type a **Project Name**.

8 Type or select a **Project Folder**.

9 Click **Next**.

10 Select a style or styles to use to create new topics.
   For example, you can create a new topic for each Heading 1 in the Word document.

11 Click **Next**.

12 Select whether you want to create new topics based on the length of your Word document. If you decide to create new topics, you can also automatically add links to the previous and next topics.

13 Click **Next**.

14 Select a stylesheet for the new topic(s).

15 Click **Next**.

16 Map your Word template (.dot) styles to your stylesheet's (.css) styles.

17 Click **Next**.

18 Map any character-level styles, like bold, to your stylesheet's styles.

19 Click **Finish**.

Importing a Word document

In RoboHelp and Flare, you can import a Word document and convert it to a topic. The process is very similar in both tools, but it's difficult to find where to begin in Flare.

To import a Word document:

1 Open the Project Organizer.

2 Right-click the **Imports** folder and select **Add MS Word Import File**.
The Add New Item dialog box appears.

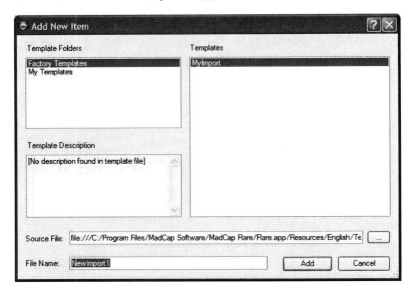

3 Select a **Template Folder** and **Template**.

4 Click **Add**.
The Import Editor appears.

5 Click **Add Files**.
The Open dialog box appears.

6 Select a Word document and click **Open**.
If needed, you can select more than one Word document.

7   If you plan to continue editing the file in Word, select **Link generated files to source files**.
    This option links the imported topics to the Word document. When you re-import the document, Flare replaces the original topics with the new topics.

8   Select the **New Topic Styles** tab.

9   Select a style or styles to use to create new topics.
    For example, you can create a new topic for each Heading 1 in the Word document.

10 Select the **Options** tab.

11 Select whether you want to create new topics based on the length of your Word document. If you decide to create new topics, you can also automatically add links to the previous and next topics.

12 Select the **Stylesheet** tab.

13 Select a stylesheet for the new topic(s).

14 Select the **Paragraph Styles** tab.

15 If needed, map (or 'convert') Word paragraph styles to Flare styles.

16 Select the **Character Styles** tab.

17 If needed, map (or 'convert') Word character styles to Flare styles.

18 Click **Import** in the toolbar.
    The Accept Imported Documents dialog box appears.

19 Click **Accept**.
    The imported topic or topics appear in the Content Explorer in a folder named after the Word import file that you used.

Importing HTML, XHTML, and XML files

Any HTML, XHTML, or XML files that are stored in your Content folder automatically appear in your project. Flare will convert HTML files to XHTML when you open them.

> *Unlike RoboHelp, Flare v1.0 cannot import Acrobat .pdf files or FrameMaker .mif files. If you need to import an Acrobat or FrameMaker file, save your file as HTML and import the HTML file.*

As mentioned on page 19 (see 'What about FrameMaker and Acrobat files?'), MadCap plans to support FrameMaker .fm file importing and exporting and .pdf exporting to Flare v2.0.

To import an HTML file:

1 In Windows Explorer, find the file that you want to import.

2 Copy the file.

3 Open your Flare project folder.

4 Open the Content folder.
If you want to import the file into a subfolder, open the subfolder.

5 Paste the file.
The file appears in the Content Explorer.

6 If you imported an HTML file, Flare will convert it to XHTML when you open it.

Images and videos

Flare and RoboHelp allow you to add .bmp, .gif, .jpg, .tif, and .png image files or .swf video files to your topics.

Shortcut	Toolbar	Menu
none	(XML Editor toolbar)	Insert > Insert Picture

Inserting an image or video

Although Flare does not include an image gallery like RoboHelp, it does provide additional options to make it easier for you to find an image or video. For example, Flare allows you to view a list of recently-viewed images, images in the current folder, or images in the My Pictures folder. Another new feature is Flare's Image Viewer. You can use the Image Viewer to preview images and watch videos.

To insert an image or video:

1 Open a topic.

2 In the XML Editor, place your insertion point cursor where you want to insert the image or video.

3 Click in the XML Editor toolbar.
  —OR—
  Select **Insert** > **Insert Picture**.

The Insert Picture dialog box appears.

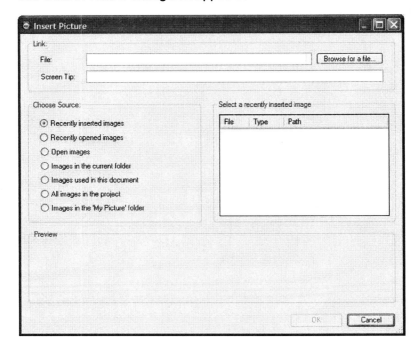

4   Click **Browse for a file** and select an image or video file.
    —OR—
    In the **File** field, type the path to the image or video file.
    —OR—
    Use one of the shortcut options in the **Choose Source** section.

5   Type a **Screen Tip**.
    Screen tips are recommended by accessibility guidelines such as the US Government's Section 508 and the W3C's Web Content Accessibility Guidelines (WCAG).

6   Click **OK**.
    The image or video appears in your topic.

'How do I see which files use an image or video?'

In RoboHelp, you can view an image or video file's properties to see which topics include the image or video. In Flare, you can right-click an image or video file and select **Show Dependencies**. In fact, you can right-click any file, including stylesheets, topics, and JavaScript files, to see its dependencies.

Links

Inserting a link in Flare is very similar to inserting a link in RoboHelp. In fact, both applications use the same toolbar icon! The only difference is that Flare's Insert Hyperlink icon appears in the XML Editor's local toolbar rather than the global toolbar.

Like RoboHelp, Flare allows you to create links to:

- Topics
- Bookmarks in topics
- Documents such as .doc, .xls, and .pdf files
- Websites
- Email addresses

'Where's the link view?'

Flare does not have a graphical link view like RoboHelp. However, you can view a list of links by right-clicking a topic and selecting **Show Dependencies**.

If you Ctrl-click a link in the XML Editor, the linked topic opens in as a new tab in the XML Editor.

Creating links

Shortcut	Toolbar	Menu
Ctrl+K	(XML Editor toolbar)	Insert > Insert Hyperlink
		Insert > Insert Topic Popup

To create a link to a topic:

1 Open the topic that will contain the link.

2 Highlight the text that you want to use as the link.
—OR—
Click an image and select **Select**.

3 Click ![icon] in the XML Editor toolbar.
—OR—
Select **Insert** > **Insert Hyperlink**.
—OR—
Press **Ctrl+K**.
The Insert Hyperlink dialog box appears.

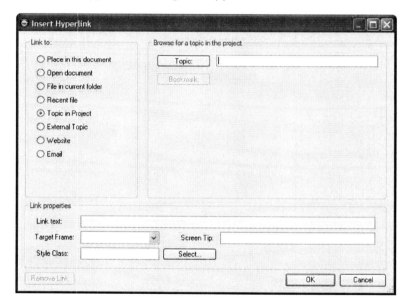

4 In the **Link to** section, select **Topic in Project**.

5 Click **Topic**.
The Link to Topic dialog box appears.

6 Select a topic.

7 Click **Open**.

70 | Links

8   Select a **Target frame**.
    The target frame specifies where the link will appear. For example, you can select 'New Window' to open the link in a new window. By default, the link will replace the current topic.

9   Type a **Screen tip**.
    Screen tips are recommended by accessibility guidelines such as Section 508 of the U.S Government's Rehabilitation Act and the W3C's Web Content Accessibility Guidelines (WCAG).

10 If needed, select a **Style Class** for the link.

11 Click **OK**.
    The hyperlink is added to the topic.

To create a link to a document:

1   Locate the document to which you want to link.

2   Copy the document to the Content folder.

3   Open the topic that will contain the link.

4   Highlight the text that you want to use as the link.
    —OR—
    Click an image and select **Select**.

5   Click in the XML Editor toolbar.
    —OR—
    Select **Insert** > **Insert Hyperlink**.
    —OR—
    Press **Ctrl+K**.

Links | 71

The Insert Hyperlink dialog box appears.

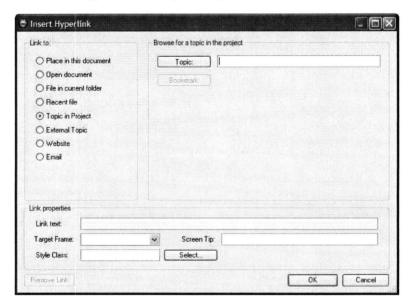

6   In the **Link to** section, select **External Topic**.

7   Click **External File**.
    The Open dialog box appears.

8   Change the file type to **All Files (*.*)**.

9   Select a file and click **Open**.

10 Select a **Target frame**.
    Links to documents often appear in a new window.

11 Type a **Screen Tip**.
    Screen tips are recommended by accessibility guidelines such as Section 508 of the U.S Government's Rehabilitation Act and the W3C's Web Content Accessibility Guidelines (WCAG).

12 If needed, select a **Style Class** for the link.

13 Click **OK**.
    The hyperlink is added to the topic.

To create a link to a website:

1 Open the topic that will contain the link.

2 Highlight the text that you want to use as the link.
—OR—
Click an image and select **Select**.

3 Click ![icon] in the XML Editor toolbar.
—OR—
Select **Insert** > **Insert Hyperlink**.
—OR—
Press **Ctrl+K**.
The Insert Hyperlink dialog box appears.

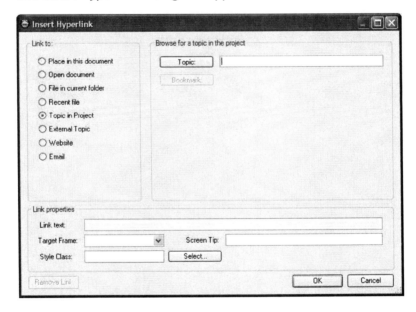

4 In the **Link to** section, select **Website**.

5 Type a website address.

6 Select a **Target Frame**.
Links to websites often appear in a new window.

7 Type a **Screen Tip**.
Screen tips are recommended by accessibility guidelines such

as Section 508 of the U.S Government's Rehabilitation Act and the W3C's Web Content Accessibility Guidelines (WCAG).

8   If needed, select a **Style Class** for the link.

9   Click **OK**.
    The hyperlink is added to the topic.

To create an image map link:

1   Open the topic that contains the picture to which you want to add links.

2   Click the image and select **Image Map**.
    The Image Map Editor window appears.

3   If the image appears faded, click .

4   Select an image map shape.

5   Draw your image map.

6   In the **Link to** section, select a link target type, such as a topic or website.
    The options on the right will change based on your selection.

7   Provide the link target information.

8   Select a **Target Frame**.

9   Type a **Screen Tip**.
    Screen tips are recommended by accessibility guidelines such as Section 508 of the U.S Government's Rehabilitation Act and the W3C's Web Content Accessibility Guidelines (WCAG).

10 Click **OK**.

11 Click **OK** in the toolbar.
    The Image Map Editor closes, and the image map is added to your image.

Popup links

Like RoboHelp, Flare can be used to add topic popups and text popups. The steps are almost identical between RoboHelp and Flare, but Flare adds a cool fade-in effect—check it out!

'What about custom-sized popups?'

You cannot create custom-sized popups in Flare like you can in RoboHelp, and imported custom-sized popups are converted to auto-sized popups. However, Flare does a better job of sizing auto-sized popups than RoboHelp.

Creating a topic popup link

Shortcut	Toolbar	Menu
Ctrl+K	(XML Editor toolbar)	Insert > Insert Topic Popup

To create a topic popup link:

1. Open the topic that will contain the link.

2. Highlight the text that you want to use as the link.
   —OR—
   Click an image and select **Select**.

3. Click in the XML Editor toolbar.
   —OR—
   Select **Insert** > **Insert Topic Popup**.
   —OR—
   Press **Ctrl+K**.

The Insert Topic Popup dialog box appears.

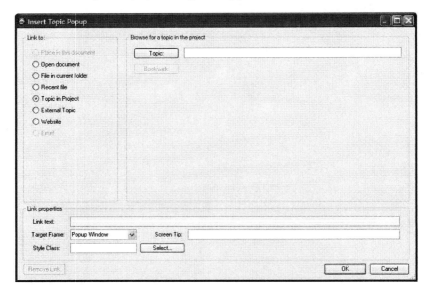

4 In the **Link to** section, select an option.

5 Select a link target.

6 Select **Popup window** as the **Target Frame**.

7 Type a **Screen tip**.
   Screen tips are recommended by accessibility guidelines such as Section 508 of the U.S Government's Rehabilitation Act and the W3C's Web Content Accessibility Guidelines (WCAG).

8 If needed, select a **Style class** for the link.

9 Click **OK**.
   The hyperlink is added to the topic.

Creating a text popup link

Unlike RoboHelp's text-only popups, Flare's text popups can only display unformatted text. You also cannot specify a background color in Flare. However, imported text popups retain their formatting and include their background color.

Shortcut	Toolbar	Menu
none	none	Insert > Insert Text Popup

To create a text popup link:

1 Open the topic that will contain the link.

2 Highlight the text that you want to use as the link.
—OR—
Click on an image and select **Select**.

3 Select **Insert** > **Insert Text Popup**.
The Insert Text Popup dialog box appears.

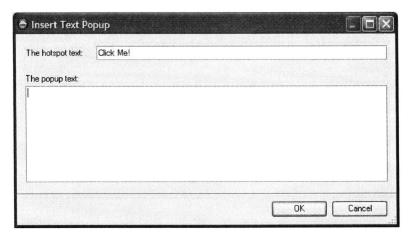

4 Type the popup text.

5 Click **OK**.
The popup link appears.

Popup links | 77

Drop-down, expanding, and toggler links

In RoboHelp, you can create drop-down and expanding navigation links. Flare adds a third type of navigation link called a 'toggler.' Flare's navigation links can also include expanded/collapsed arrow icons, so users know if a drop-down, expanding, or toggler navigation link is open or closed.

'What is the difference?'

A **drop-down** link shows and hides a paragraph, image, or list item *below* the drop-down link. Drop-down links are often used to show and hide content between subheadings.

An **expanding** link shows and hides a word or sentence *within* a paragraph or list item. Expanding links are often used to show and hide short definitions.

A **toggler** link shows and hides a named paragraph, image, or list item (or multiple items with the same name) *anywhere* in the topic. Toggler links are often used to show and hide a screenshot or table from a link at the top of a topic.

Creating a drop-down link

Shortcut	Toolbar	Menu
none	none	Insert > Insert Drop-Down Text

To create a drop-down link:

1 Open the topic that will contain the drop-down link.

2 Type and highlight the drop-down link and drop-down text.

3 Select **Insert > Insert Drop-Down Text**.
   The Insert Drop-Down dialog box appears.

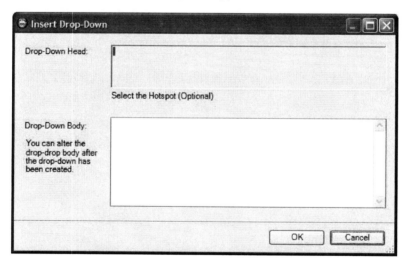

4 Highlight the text you want to use as the drop-down link (or 'head').

5 Click **OK**.
   The ⬇ drop-down icon appears to the left of the drop-down link.

80 | Drop-down, expanding, and toggler links

Creating an expanding link

Shortcut	Toolbar	Menu
none	none	Insert > Insert Expanding Text

To create an expanding link:

1 Open the topic that will contain the expanding text link.

2 Highlight the expanding link and text.

3 Select **Insert** > **Insert Expanding Text**.
The Insert Expanding Text dialog box.

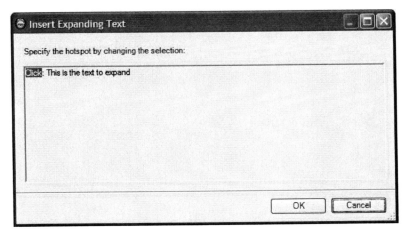

4 Highlight the text that you want to use as the link.

5 Click **OK**.
The [T] expanding text link icon appears after the expanding text link.

Creating a toggler link NEW!

Shortcut	Toolbar	Menu
none	none	Insert > Insert Toggler

To create a toggler link:

1 Open the topic that will contain the toggler link.

2 Click inside or highlight the toggler content block.

3 If the tag block bars are not displayed to the left of the topic, click ▦ in the XML Editor toolbar.

4 Click the tag bar next to the content that you want to toggle.

5 In the popup menu, select **Name**.

6 Type a name for the toggled element.

7 Click **OK**.

8 If needed, assign the same name to other content blocks.

9 In the topic, highlight the text that you want to use as the toggler link.

10 Select **Insert** > **Insert Toggler**.

The Insert Toggler dialog box appears.

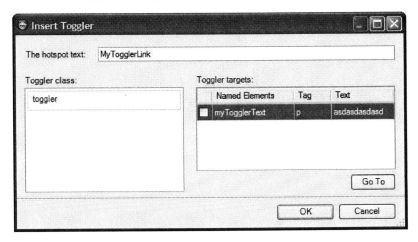

11 Select a toggler target by checking its checkbox.
Remember, you can associate more than one target with a toggler link.

12 Click **OK**.
The 🔲 toggler icon appears to the left of the toggler text.

Drop-down, expanding, and toggler links | **83**

Related topics, keyword, and concept links

In RoboHelp and Flare, you can add related topics, keyword, and see also links. However, Flare uses the more descriptive 'concept links' name for see also links. The steps for creating related topics, keyword, and concept links are very similar in RoboHelp and Flare.

'What is the difference?'

All three of these links open a popup list of topics. The difference between them is how you select the topics that appear in the list.

Related topics links display a list of topics that you have manually selected. They are easier to create than keyword and concept links, but they are much harder to update. If you need to update a related topics link, you have to manually add topics to or remove topics from the list.

Keyword links display a list of topics that include the same index term (or 'keyword'). If you remove a keyword from or add a keyword to a topic, all of the keyword links that use the keyword are automatically updated.

Concept links display a list of topics that include the same concept term. If you remove a concept term from or add a concept term to a topic, all of the concept links that use that concept term are automatically updated.

Creating a related topics link

Shortcut	Toolbar	Menu
none	none	Insert > Insert Help Control > Related Topics Control

To create a related topic link:

1 Open the topic that will contain the related topics link.

2 Position your cursor where you want to insert the related topics link.

3 Select **Insert** > **Insert Help Control** > **Related Topics Control**. The Insert Related Topics Control dialog box appears.

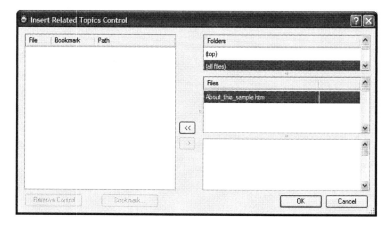

4 Select the **Folder** that contains the topic.

5 Select a topic in the **Files** section.

6 Click <<< to add the topic to the related topics link.

7 Add more topics as needed.

8 Click **OK**.
The related topics link appears in your topic.

Creating a keyword link

Shortcut	Toolbar	Menu
none	none	Insert > Insert Help Control > Keyword Link Control

To create a keyword link:

1 Open the topic that will contain the keyword link.

2 Position your cursor where you want to insert the keyword link.

3 Select **Insert** > **Insert Help Control** > **Keyword Link Control**.
The Insert Keyword Link Control dialog box appears.

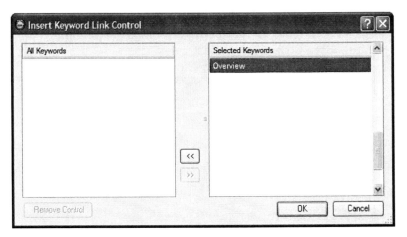

4 Select a keyword.

5 Click <<< to add the keyword to the keyword link.

6 Add more keywords as needed.

7 Click **OK**.
The keyword link appears in your topic.

Keyword links do not work in the preview, but they work great in DotNet Help, HTML Help, and WebHelp.

Creating a concept link

Before you create a concept link, you need to add concept terms to your topics. When you create a concept link, you select the concept term to include all of the topics associated with the term.

In RoboHelp, see also groups are hidden on the Index tab. Flare provides a Concept Entry window to make adding concept terms much easier.

Shortcut	Toolbar	Menu
none	none	Insert > Insert Help Control > Concept Link

To add a concept term:

1 Open a topic to associate with the concept term.

2 Position the cursor where you want to add the concept term.

3 Select **Tools** > **Concepts** > **Concept Entry Window**.
—OR—
Press **Shift+F9**.

The Concept Entry window appears.

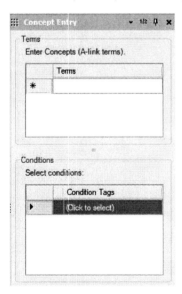

88 | Related topic, keyword, and concept links

4 Type a concept term and press **Enter**.

5 Type more terms as needed.

6 Click **Save**.

To add a concept link:

1 Open the topic that will contain the concept link.

2 Position your cursor where you want to insert the concept link.

3 Select **Insert** > **Insert Help Control** > **Concept Link**.

The Insert Concept Link Control dialog box appears.

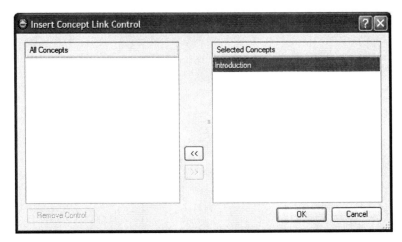

4 Select a concept term.

5 Click <<< to add the concept term to the concept link.

6 Click **OK**.
The concept link is added to the topic.

◇ *Concept links do not work in the preview, but they work great in DotNet Help, HTML Help, and WebHelp.*

Related topic, keyword, and concept links | **89**

Browse sequences

In Flare, browse sequences look like TOCs. Imported RoboHelp browse sequences resemble TOC books, and browse sequence topics resemble TOC pages.

Creating a browse sequence

Shortcut	Toolbar	Menu
none	none	Project > Advanced > Add Browse Sequence

To create a browse sequence:

1 Select **Project > Advanced > Add Browse Sequence**.
   The Add New Item dialog box appears.

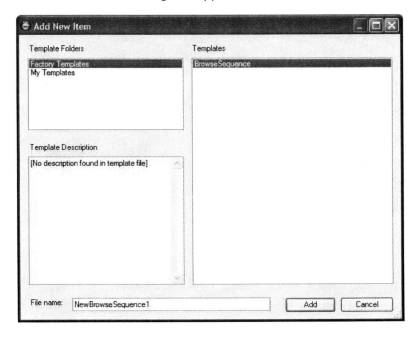

2 Select a **Template Folder** and **Template**.

3 Type a **File name** for the browse sequence.
Browse sequences have a .flbrs extension. If you don't type the extension, Flare will add it for you.

4 Click **Add** and click **OK**.
The browse sequence appears in the Advanced folder in the Project Organizer and opens in the Browse Sequence Editor.

To add books to a browse sequence:

1 Open the browse sequence.

2 Open the Content Explorer.

3 Drag a folder from the Content Explorer to the browse sequence.

4 If you need to rename the browse sequence book, click the selected new book entry.
—OR—
Press **F2**.
The text for the entry is now highlighted.

Type the new name.

To manually add books to a browse sequence:

1 Open the browse sequence.

2 Click ▭ or ▭ in the Browse Sequence Editor toolbar.
A book named 'New TOC Book' is added to the browse sequence.

3 Click the selected new book entry.
—OR—
Press **F2**.
The text for the entry is now highlighted.

Type a name for the book.

To add pages to a browse sequence using drag-and-drop:

1 Open the browse sequence.

2 Open the Content Explorer.

3 Drag a topic from the Content Explorer to the browse sequence.

4 If necessary, use the arrows in the browse sequence toolbar to move the page up, down, left or right.

To add pages to a browse sequence using the Browse Sequence Editor:

1 Open the browse sequence.

2 Select the location in the browse sequence where you want to add the new entry.

3 Click in the Browse Sequence Editor.
An entry named 'New entry' is added to the browse sequence.

4 Click the selected new entry.
—OR—
Press **F2**.
The text for the entry is now highlighted.

5 Type a name for the entry and press **Enter**.

6 If necessary, use the arrow buttons in the browse sequence toolbar to move the page left, right, up, or down.

7 Double-click the new entry.

The Properties dialog box appears.

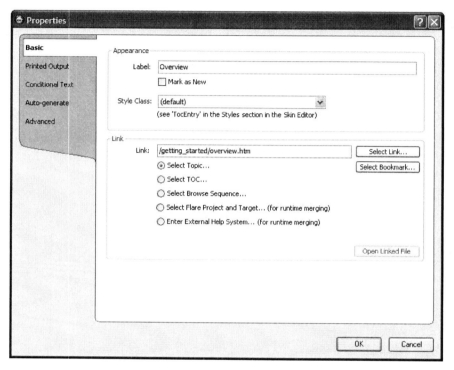

8 If needed, select the **Mark as New** option.

The page will be marked with the 'New' icon:

9 Select **Select Topic**.

10 Click **Select Link**.

The Link to Topic dialog box appears.

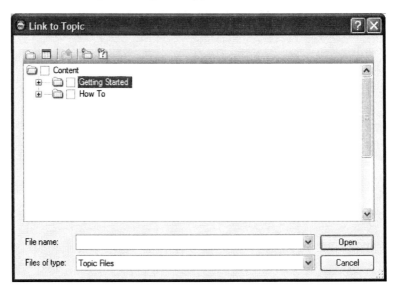

11 Select a topic and click **Open**.

12 Click **OK**.

Creating a browse sequence based on your TOC 💡

In RoboHelp, you can auto-create a browse sequence based on your TOC. Flare does not have an auto-create feature, but you *can* create a browse sequence based on your TOC.

To create a browse sequence based on your TOC:

1 In Windows Explorer, create a copy of your TOC file.
By default, TOC files are located in the Project\TOCs folder.

2 Paste the copy of your TOC file into the Project\Advanced folder.

3 Change the TOC file's extension from .fltoc to .flbrs.
The Rename dialog box appears.

Browse sequences | 95

4 Click **Yes**.

Your new browse sequence appears in the Advanced folder in the Project Organizer.

Using a browse sequence

To use a browse sequence, you need to enable it in a skin and associate it with a target. You can use different browse sequences in different targets, or you can use multiple browse sequences in the same target.

To enable a browse sequence in a skin:

1 Open a skin.

2 On the Basic tab, select the **Browse Sequence** checkbox.

To associate a browse sequence with a target:

1 Open a target.

2 On the Basic tab, make sure the browse sequence is enabled in the selected skin.

3 Select a **Browse Sequence**.

'Where are my HTML Help browse sequences?'

RoboHelp uses a .dll file named 'ActiveX.dll' to add a browse sequence area to HTML Help. Flare does not require any .dll files for HTML Help. Instead, your browse sequences appear at the bottom of your TOC and the selected topic opens on the right in the topic pane.

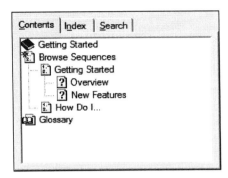

TOCs

Flare and RoboHelp allow you to link your TOC books and pages to topics, bookmarks inside of topics, websites, email addresses, a document such as a .doc, .xls, or .pdf file, or a topic in another help system. However, Flare allows you to have multiple TOCs, and you can link a book or page in one TOC to another TOC. You can also link a book or page to a browse sequence.

'Where's the TOC file?'

In RoboHelp, your TOC is stored in a .hhc file. In Flare, it's stored in an XML-based .fltoc file.

Making Flare look like RoboHelp: docking the TOC

You can move the TOC Editor to the Document Dock to make Flare look more like RoboHelp. You can even Ctrl-click a book or page in the TOC to open its associated topic in the XML Editor.

Shortcut	Toolbar	Menu
none	none	Window > Send to Other Dock

To dock the TOC Editor:

1. Open your TOC in the TOC Editor.
2. Select **Window** > **Send to Other Dock**.
   Your TOC will move to the left dock.

Manually creating a TOC

Flare and RoboHelp both provide manual and automatic ways to create a TOC. The manual approach is the same in both applications: click the new book or new page icon, type a title, and select a link (selecting a link is optional for books). Or, you can drag a topic from the Topics tab (RoboHelp) or Content Explorer (Flare) to the TOC. In Flare you can even drag a folder to the TOC and auto-create a book for the folder and pages for each topic inside the book.

To create a TOC book:

1. Click ▢ in the toolbar.
   —OR—
   Press **Ctrl+F8**.
   The master TOC appears in the TOC Editor.

2. Click ▢ in the TOC Editor toolbar.
   A new TOC book named **New TOC Book** appears.

3. Click the new TOC book.

4. Type a name for the book.

5. If necessary, move the book to a new location in the TOC. You can drag-and-drop the TOC book or use the arrows in the TOC Editor toolbar.

To create a TOC page:

1. Open the TOC.

2. If you want to add a page inside a book, select the book.

3. Click ▢ in the TOC Editor toolbar.
   A new TOC page named New Entry appears.

4. Double-click the TOC page.
   —OR—

Click ![icon] in the TOC Editor toolbar.
The Properties dialog box appears.

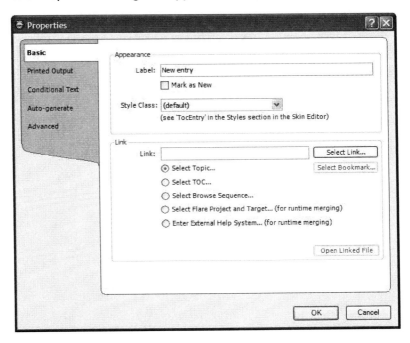

5   Type a **Label** for the page.

6   Click **Select link**.
    The Link to Topic dialog box appears.

7   Select a topic.

8   Click **Open**.

9   Click **OK**.

Auto-generating a TOC

Flare's 'Auto-generate TOC' option is very different from RoboHelp's 'auto-create TOC' command. In RoboHelp, you can auto-create a TOC to match your Project tab: folders become TOC books and topics become TOC pages.

In Flare, you can auto-generate a TOC entry based on the heading structure in a topic. For example, the following topic has one main heading and four sub-headings:

> **South Africa** (formatted as Heading 1)
> *Cape Town* (Heading 2)
> *Durban* (Heading 2)
> *Johannesburg* (Heading 2)
> *Pretoria* (Heading 2)

You can auto-create the following TOC entries for this topic:

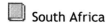 South Africa

    📄 Cape Town
    📄 Durban
    📄 Johannesburg
    📄 Pretoria

To auto-generate TOC entries:

1   Double-click a TOC page.
    The Properties dialog box appears.

2   Select the **Auto-generate** tab.

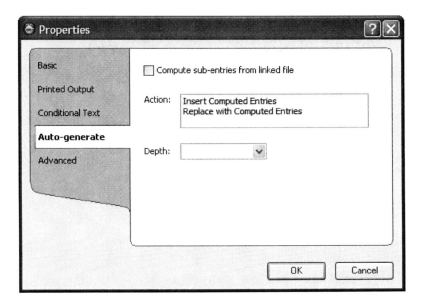

3 Select **Compute sub-entries from linked file**.

4 Select an **Action**.

- **Insert Computed Entries** adds the TOC entries below the selected TOC entry.

- **Replace with Computed Entries** replaces the selected TOC entry with the new entries.

5 Select a heading **Depth**.

6 Click **OK**.

Creating multiple TOCs NEW!

Flare makes it easy to share content across projects. For example, you might want to use the same troubleshooting topics in all of your help systems. You can create a TOC named 'Troubleshooting' that contains pages for all of the troubleshooting topics. You can then import these topics and their TOC into each help system.

Shortcut	Toolbar	Menu
none	none	Project > Add Table of Contents

To create a TOC:

1. Select **Project > Add Table of Contents**.
   —OR—
   Right-click the TOCs folder and select **Add Table of Contents**. The Add TOC dialog box appears.

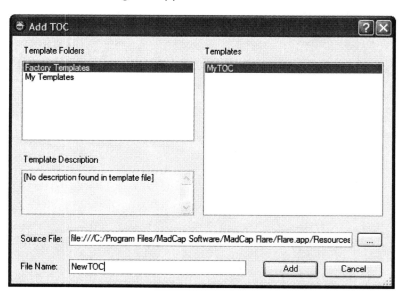

2. Select a **Template Folder** and **Template**.
3. Type a **File Name**.

4   Click **Add**.

    The TOC appears in the TOC folder in the Project Organizer and opens in the TOC Editor.

Linking TOCs NEW!

If you create multiple TOCs, you can create a link from the 'master' TOC to the other TOCs.

To link TOCs:

1   Open your TOC.

2   Select the location in the TOC where you want to add the link to the other TOC.

3   Click .

    A new TOC entry named 'New entry' appears.

4   Select the new entry and click .

    The Properties dialog box appears.

5   Click **Select TOC**.

    The Link to TOC dialog box appears.

6   Select the TOC to which you want to link the page.

7   Click **Open**.

8   Click **OK**.

    The icon in the TOC Editor changes to , indicating that the page is linked to a TOC.

Associating a TOC with a target

If you have multiple TOCs, you need to associate one of your TOCs with your target. For example, you could create a TOC to create help for experts, one for beginners, one for Sales team members, and one for printed documentation.

If you only have one TOC, Flare will automatically associate it with your targets.

To associate a TOC with a target:

1 Open the target.

2 On the Basic tab, select a **Master TOC**.

Indexes

Indexing is very different between RoboHelp and Flare. In RoboHelp, you can add keywords to topics (as meta tags) or to an external .hhk file. In Flare, you always add your keywords to topics.

Unlike RoboHelp, Flare adds your keywords inside your content rather than to the <head> section as meta tags. You can copy a keyword to other topics or delete a keyword when you delete its associated content.

Flare does not include an index wizard like RoboHelp. However, Flare provides three different methods for adding index entries:

- 'Quick term' method
- Index Entry Window method
- Index Entry Mode method

NEW! In Flare, you can assign a conditional tag to an index entry. If you exclude the conditional tag when you build a target, the index entry is removed from the index.

'What about my RoboHelp index?'

When you import a RoboHelp project, Flare adds your index keywords before the exact word (or words) in the topic. If an index keyword does not exactly match any words in the topic, the keyword is added to the beginning of the topic. When the user selects a keyword in the index, the topic opens to where the index keyword is placed in the topic.

Shortcut	Toolbar	Menu
F9		Tools > Index > Insert <term> as Index Keyword
		Tools > Index > Index Entry Window

Adding index entries using the 'quick term' method

The quick term method can be used to quickly add a term to the index while you are writing. Because it's so efficient, I normally use the quick term method to add index terms.

The quick term method can only be used to add single-word index entries. If you need to add a multiple word index entry or a second-level entry, you will need to use the Index Entry window or Index Entry mode.

To add a term using the quick term method:

1. Open a topic.

2. Click before or on the word that you want to insert as an index term.

3. Select **Tools** > **Index** > **Insert <term> as Index Keyword**. The term is added to the index. If you have Show Markers turned on, the term will appear in a green box.

   To show markers, click <t> *in the XML Editor toolbar and select* **Show Markers**. *If you can't see the entire index entry, adjust the Marker Width.*

Adding index entries using the Index Entry window method

The Index Entry window can be used to add single word, multiple word, and second-level index entries. The Index Entry window shows all of the index terms within the current topic.

To add an index entry using the Index Entry window:

1. Open a topic.

2. Click before or on the word or phrase that you want to insert as an index term.

3   Select **Tools** > **Index** > **Index Entry Window**.
    —OR—
    Press **F9**.
    The Index Entry window appears.

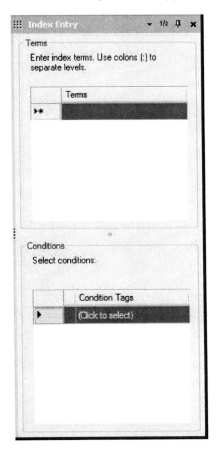

4   Type a term or phrase and press **Enter**.
    The term or phrase is added to the index.

Adding index entries using the Index Entry mode method NEW!

Index Entry mode is useful when you need to add multiple index entries at once. When you switch to Index Entry mode, the words you type become index entries rather than topic content. It's a great tool for indexers, since they can focus on indexing and not worry about accidentally changing the content in a topic.

To add an index entry using Index Entry mode:

1   Open a topic.

2   Click ![] in the XML Editor toolbar.

3   Position the cursor where you want to add the index term.

4   Type the term and press **Enter**.
    The Index Entry window appears, and the term is added to the index.

5   Continue typing terms as needed. When you are done, click ![] in the XML Editor.

Showing or hiding index entries in a topic

Index entry markers can be distracting when you are not indexing a topic. You can hide the index markers using the Show Tags icon in the XML Editor's toolbar.

To show or hide index markers:

1   Click the ![] icons' down arrow.

2   Select **Show Markers**.
    The index markers disappear.

   TIP> *You can change the size of the markers by modifying the Marker Width setting.*

Viewing the index

Select **View** > **Index Explorer** to view the index. The Index Explorer is similar to RoboHelp's Index tab. It displays all of the index entries and their associated topics. Unlike RoboHelp's Index tab, you cannot use Flare's Index Explorer to add new terms.

Glossaries

RoboHelp and Flare both provide two glossary features: a glossary tab/page and glossary links. Users can see a list of terms on the glossary page, or they can view a definition from within a topic by clicking a glossary link.

When you create a glossary link in RoboHelp, the definition is copied to your topic. If you change the definition, you have to update all of the glossary links. Another downside is that glossary links use expanding text, so the definition appears within the sentence. These expanding text can be hard to read. A final issue is that RoboHelp's glossary definitions can only contain unformatted text. Flare fixes all of these problems!

With Flare, you can create expanding, drop-down, or popup glossary hotspots. Your terms are also dynamic—if you change the definition in the glossary, the new definition will automatically display from your links. You can even associate a term with a topic, which means your glossary terms can contain any type of content, including formatted text, images, or videos.

Glossary terms are stored in a glossary file with a .flglo extension. Glossary files are stored in the Glossaries subfolder in the Project folder.

Creating a glossary

You can use multiple glossaries in a project. For example, you can maintain a glossary of common terms that are shared across multiple projects. You can then store your project-specific terms in a project glossary.

Shortcut	Toolbar	Menu
none		Project > Add Glossary

To create a glossary:

1. Select **Project** > **Add Glossary**.
   The Add New Item dialog box appears.

2. Select a **Template Folder** and **Template**.

3. Type a **File name**.
   Glossaries have a .flglo extension. If you don't type the extension, Flare will add it for you.

4. Click **Add**.
   The glossary appears in the Glossaries folder in the Project Organizer and opens in the Glossary Editor.

Making Flare look like RoboHelp: moving the glossary TIP

You can move the Glossary Editor to the left pane to look like RoboHelp's Glossary tab.

1. Open a glossary.

2. Select **Window** > **Floating**.

3. Click the window's title bar, drag it to the left side of the Flare window, and drop it on the bull's eye. The Glossary Editor is now docked in the left pane.

   The left pane can only show four accordion items. If you add more than four accordion items, the additional items appear as buttons.

Adding terms to a glossary

You can add terms directly to a glossary. When you build a target (such as WebHelp), you can automatically create glossary links for the first appearance of a term in a topic or for every appearance of a term in a topic.

1. Open a glossary.
   Glossaries are stored in the Glossaries folder in the Project Organizer.

2. Click ![icon] in the Glossary Editor toolbar.
   The Properties dialog box appears.

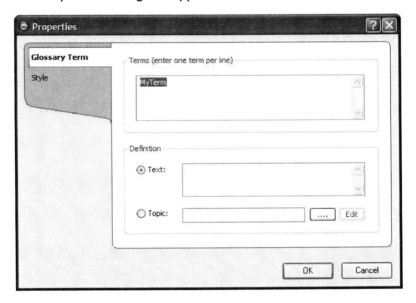

3. Type a glossary term.
4. Type a definition or select a topic that contains the definition.
5. Select the **Style** tab.

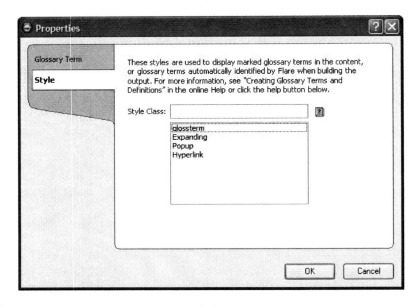

6   Select a style for the glossary link:

- **glossterm** — opens the definition based on the glossterm style (which you can customize)
- **Expanding** — opens the definition with an expanding link
- **Popup** — opens the definition in a popup window
- **Hyperlink** — closes the current topic and opens the glossary page

If you do not select a style, Flare uses the 'Popup' style.

7   Click **OK**.

Inserting glossary links for new terms

You can add glossary terms and links as you are writing your topics.

1. Open a topic.
2. Highlight the word or phrase that will become the glossary link.
3. Select **Insert** > **Insert Glossary Term Link**.
   The Create Glossary Term dialog box appears.

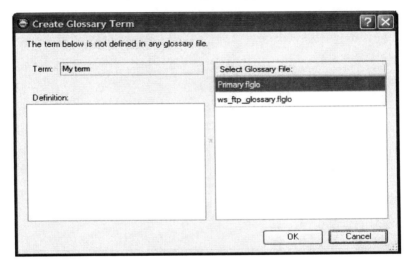

4. Select a **Glossary file**.
5. Type a definition.
6. Click **OK**.

Inserting glossary links for existing terms

1 Open a topic.

2 Position the cursor where you want to insert the glossary link.

3 Select **Tools** > **Glossary Terms**.
   The Glossary window appears.

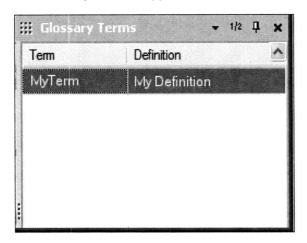

4 Double-click the term that you want to insert into the topic.
   Be sure to double-click the term. If you double-click anywhere else, the Glossary Editor opens.
   The term appears in the topic as a glossary link.

Using a glossary

To use a glossary, you need to enable it in a skin and associate it with a target. You can use different glossaries in different targets, or you can use multiple glossaries in the same target.

To enable a glossary in a skin:

1 Open a skin.

2 On the Basic tab, select the **Glossary** checkbox.

To associate a glossary with a target:

1 Open a target.

2 Select the **Glossary** tab.

3 Select a **Glossary Term Conversion** method.

4 Select a **Glossary File**.

5 Click **Save**.

'Where's the HTML Help glossary tab?'

RoboHelp uses a .dll file named 'ActiveX.dll' to display a glossary tab in HTML Help. Flare does not require any .dll files for HTML Help. Instead, your glossary appears at the bottom of your TOC and opens on the right in the topic pane.

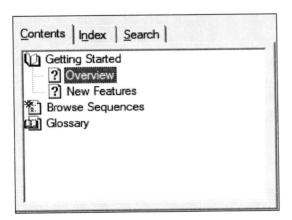

Stylesheets

Creating and applying stylesheets and styles are very similar tasks in RoboHelp and Flare. However, Flare adds some great new style features:

- **Medium types** — you can specify different style attributes for different media types, such as print and online
- **Multiple stylesheets** — you can associate multiple stylesheets with a topic
- **Navigation control styles** — you can modify the appearance of concept, keyword, and related topics links
- **Table stylesheets** — you can create table stylesheets to control table borders, padding and background color(s)

In Flare, stylesheets appear in the Content Explorer. Imported RoboHelp stylesheets appear in the top-level ('Content') folder. Stylesheets created in Flare appear in the Resources\Stylesheets folder. If needed, you can move a stylesheet to a different folder.

Creating a stylesheet

Although most help projects only use one stylesheet, you can create and use multiple stylesheets. For example, you could create a "New Topic" stylesheet to use for new topics.

Shortcut	Toolbar	Menu
none	none	Project > Add Stylesheet

To create a stylesheet:

1 Select **Project** > **Add Stylesheet**.

The Add New Stylesheet dialog box appears.

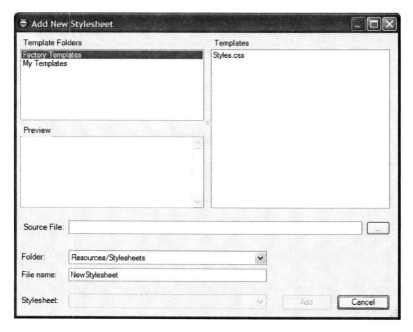

2 Select a **Template Folder** and **Template**.

3 Select a **Folder** for the stylesheet.
By default, stylesheets are stored in the Resources\Stylesheets folder.

4   Type a **File name** for the stylesheet.
    Stylesheets have a .css extension. If you don't type the extension, Flare will add it for you.

5   Click **Add**.
    The Copy to Project dialog box appears.

6   Click **OK**.
    The stylesheet appears in the Content Explorer and opens in the Stylesheet Editor.

Importing a stylesheet

Unlike snippets, variables, and topics (which can just be copied to your project folder), stylesheets must be imported into your project before you can use them.

Shortcut	Toolbar	Menu
none	none	Project > Add Stylesheet

To import a stylesheet:

1   Select **Project>Add Stylesheet**.
    The Add New Stylesheet dialog box appears.

2   Click [...] next to the **Source File** field.
    The Open dialog box appears.

3   Select the stylesheet file that you want to import and click **Open**.

4   Click **Add**.
    The Copy to Project dialog box appears.

5   Click **OK**.

Stylesheets | 123

Creating a style

You can create style classes as you write and format topics or from within the Stylesheet Editor.

To create a style:

1 Open a topic in which you want to use the new style.

2 Use the **Format** menu commands to format the text.

3 Click inside the formatted content.
   Do not highlight the content.

4 Select **View** > **Style Window**.
   —OR—
   Press **F12**.
   The Style window appears.

5 Click **Create Style**.

   The Create Style dialog box appears.

   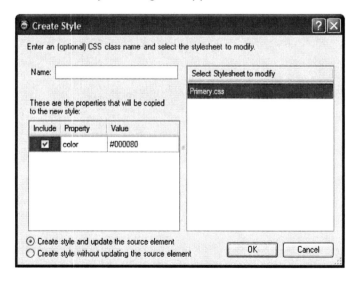

6 In the **Name** field, type a name for the new style without using spaces.

124 | Stylesheets

7   If you do not want to include a style property in the new style, remove the check from its **Include** checkbox.

8   If you want the new style to be applied to the selected content, select **Create style and update the source element**.

    If you do not want the new style to be applied to the selected content, select **Create style without updating the source element**.

9   Click **OK**.
    The new style is added to the stylesheet.

Modifying a style

You can use Flare's Stylesheet Editor to completely customize your styles.

To modify a style:

1   Open the stylesheet.

    By default, stylesheets are stored in the Resources folder in the Content Explorer.

The Stylesheet Editor appears.

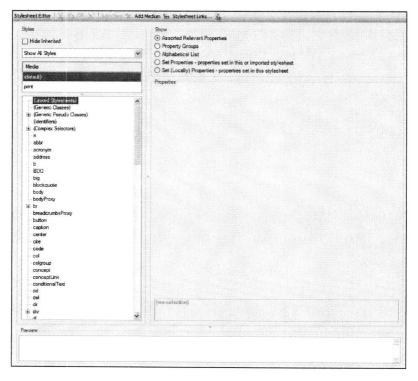

2 Select the style you want to edit.
   The selected style's properties appear on the right.

3 Select a property.

4 Select a value to change.

5 Type or select a new value.

6 Modify other properties as needed.

Creating a style medium

You can use medium types to specify different style attributes for different media, such as print and online.

To create a style medium:

1. Open your stylesheet.
   Stylesheets are stored in the Resources folder in the Content Explorer.

2. Click **Add Medium** in the Stylesheet Editor toolbar.
   The Rename Medium dialog box appears.

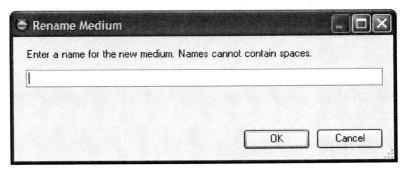

3. Type a name for the medium.
   Medium names cannot include spaces.

4. Click **OK**.
   The new medium type appears in the media section.

   If you want to change the properties of a style for a medium type:

   - Select the medium in the **Media** section.
   - Select a style.
   - Modify the style's properties.
   - Click **Save**.

Associating a topic with a stylesheet

Shortcut	Toolbar	Menu
none	none	Tools > Stylesheet Links

To associate a topic with a stylesheet:

1 Open the topic that you want to link to a stylesheet.

2 Select **Tools** > **Stylesheet Links**.

The Stylesheet Links dialog box appears.

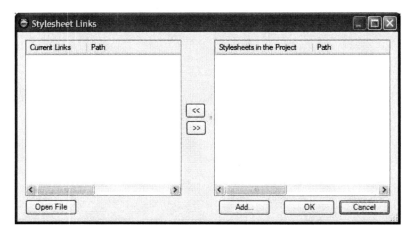

3 Select a stylesheet.

4 Click [<<].

The stylesheet is added to the list on the left.

5 Click **OK**.

The stylesheet is applied to the topic.

Associating multiple topics with a stylesheet

You probably don't want to individually associate each topic with your stylesheet. That could take a *long* time! You can assign all of the topics in a folder to a stylesheet using the Show Files button in the Content Explorer. However, you can only select topics within a folder: Flare v1.0 does not provide a way to select all files.

To associate multiple topics with a stylesheet:

1 Click in the Content Explorer toolbar.
   The Content Explorer splits into two halves (left and right).

2 On the left side of the Content Explorer, select the folder that contains the topics.

3 On the right side of the Content Explorer, select the topics. Hold **Shift** to select a range of topics or hold **Ctrl** to select individual topics.

4 Click in the Content Explorer toolbar.
   The Properties dialog box appears.

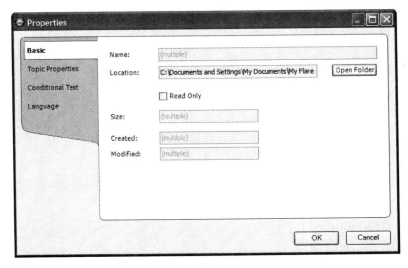

5 Select the **Topic Properties** tab.
The Topic Properties dialog appears.

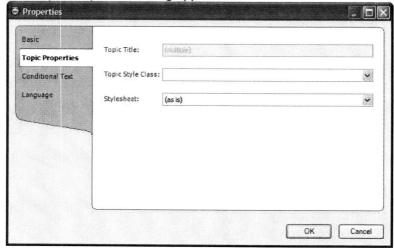

6 In the **Stylesheet** field, click the drop-down arrow and select a stylesheet.

7 Click **OK**.
The topics are associated with the stylesheet.

Master pages

In RoboHelp, you can create a topic template to include default content in a topic's header, body, or footer. In Flare, you can create a template to include default content when you create almost anything, including topics, skins, stylesheets, targets, and TOCs. If you want to add a shared header or footer to your topics, you can create a master page.

Master pages can include the following elements (Flare calls these elements 'proxies'):

- **Breadcrumbs** automatically provide a list of the TOC books above the current topic. If your books are linked to topics, the links are included in the breadcrumb trail.
- **Glossary**, **index**, and **TOC proxies** are used to include these features in printed documentation.
- **Page headers** and **footers** can be used in printed documentation master pages to add odd, even, and first page headers and footers to your printed documentation.
- A **mini-TOC** automatically adds links to the topics below the current topic.

Master pages are associated with targets, not topics. For example, you can create a master page for WebHelp that includes a mini-TOC and a master page for printed documentation that contains a footer.

'Where's my RoboHelp template?'

Flare converts headers and footers in RoboHelp templates to snippets and insert the snippets into the topics that used the template. A snippet is content that you can reuse in your topics—not just in the header or footer. For more information about snippets, see page 145.

Creating a master page

You can create as many master pages as you need. However, you can only use one master page in a target. Master pages have a .flmsp extension, and they are stored in the Resources\MasterPages folder in the Content Explorer.

Shortcut	Toolbar	Menu
none	none	Project > Add Master Page

To create a master page:

1 Select **Project > Add Master Page**.
   The Add New Master Page dialog box appears.

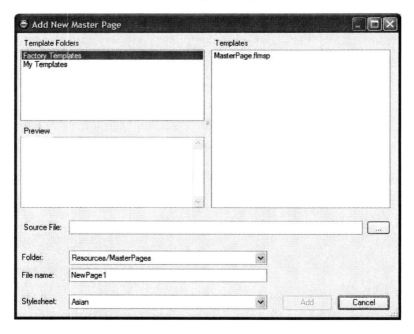

2 Select a **Template Folder** and **Template**.

3 Type a **File name**.
   Master pages have a .flmsp extension. If you don't type the extension, Flare will add it for you.

4 Select a **Stylesheet**.

5 Click **Add**.
   The Copy to Project dialog box appears.

6 Click **OK**.
   The master page appears in the Content Explorer and appears in the XML Editor.

Adding a proxy to a master page NEW!

You can add a proxy to or delete a proxy from a master page. In printed documentation, any proxies above the topic body proxy are placed in a header, and any proxies below the topic body proxy are placed in the footer.

To add a header to a master page:

1 Open the master page.

2 Position the cursor above the **topic body** proxy.

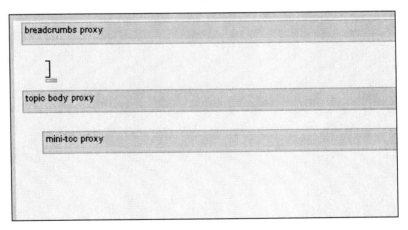

3 Type or insert your header's content.
   Headers can use styles and can include images.

To add a footer to a master page:

1 Open the master page.

2 Position the cursor below the topic body proxy.

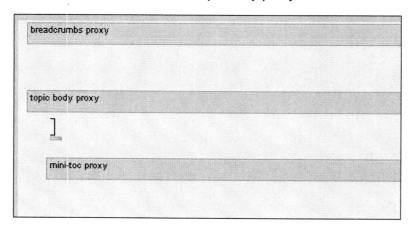

3 Type or insert your footer's text.

Footers can use styles and can include images.

Associating a master page with a target

To use a master page, you need to associate it with a target. You can associate the same master page with multiple targets, or you can associate a different master page with each of your targets.

To associate a master page with a target:

1 Open a target.

2 Select the **Advanced** tab.

3 Select a **Master Page**.

4 Click **Save**.

Skins

In RoboHelp, you use skins to customize the appearance of WebHelp and FlashHelp, and you use windows to customize the size and location of the help window. For example, if you want to have a blue background in the navigation bar, you change the skin's settings. If you want to position the help window in the top left corner, you change the window's settings. In Flare, skins control the appearance *and* size of the help window.

Skin files have a .flskn extension. They appear in the Skins folder in the Project Organizer.

'Where's the skin gallery?'

Flare does not have a built-in skin gallery, but MadCap will be posting a skin gallery on their website (www.madcapsoftware.com).

Creating a skin

You can use the same skin for all of your online help targets, or you can create different skins for each target.

Shortcut	Toolbar	Menu
none	none	Project > Add Skin

To create a skin:

1. Select **Project** > **Add Skin**.
   —OR—
   Right-click the **Skins** folder and select **Add Skin**.

2. Select a **Template Folder** and **Template**.

3. Type a **File name** for the skin.
   Skins have a .flskn extension. If you don't type the extension, Flare will add it for you.

4   Click **Add**.
    The Copy to Project dialog box appears.

5   Click **OK**.
    The skin appears in the Skins folder in the Project Organizer and opens in the Skin Editor.

Importing a skin

You can import a skin from another project so that all of your help systems have the same design.

Shortcut	Toolbar	Menu
none	none	Project > Add Skin

To import a skin:

1   Select **Project > Add Skin**.
    —OR—
    Right-click the **Skins** folder and select **Add Skin**.

2   Click [...] to find a skin file to import.
    The Open dialog box appears.

3   Locate and select a skin file.

4   Click **Open**.

5   Click **Add**.
    The imported skin appears in the Skins folder in the Project Organizer and opens in the Skin Editor.

Editing a skin

You can edit a skin to change the size, appearance, and features used in your online help.

To edit a skin:

1. Open the skin.

    The skin appears in the Skin Editor.

    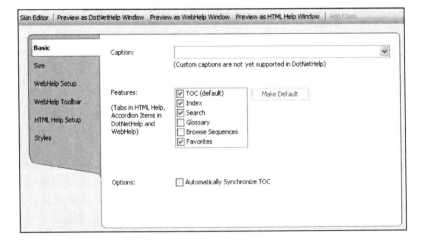

2. On the Basic tab, type a **Caption**.
    The caption appears in the help window's title bar.

3. Select the **Features** that you want to appear in the help window.

4. Enable or disable **Automatically Synchronize TOC**.

5. Select the **Size** tab.

6. Type values for the window positions.
    —OR—
    Click **Preview Full Size**, resize the preview window, and click **OK**.

7   If you are editing a WebHelp skin:
    □   Select the **WebHelp Setup** tab.
    □   Type a **Navigation Pane Size**.
        If you type **0**, Flare will automatically size the navigation pane.
    □   Select a **Navigation Pane Position**.
    □   Select the number of **Visible Accordion Items** you would like to use.
    □   Select an **About Box Bitmap** image.
    □   Select the **WebHelp Toolbar Setup** tab.
    □   Select the **WebHelp Toolbar Buttons** you want to include.
8   If you are editing an HTML Help skin:
    □   Click the **HTML Help Setup** tab.
    □   Select the **HTML Help Buttons** you want to include.
    □   Select the **Button**, **Navigation Pane**, and **Misc Options** you want to use.
9   Select the **Styles** tab.
10 Modify the skin styles as needed.
11 Click **Save**.

Associating a skin with a target

To use a skin, you need to associate it with a target. You can associate the same skin with multiple targets, or you can associate a different skins with each target.

To associate a skin with a target:

1   Open a target.
2   On the Basic tab, select a **Skin**.
3   Click **Save**.

Variables and snippets

In RoboHelp, the only way to reuse the same content in multiple topics is to place it in a template's header or footer. When you attach your topics to the template, RoboHelp adds the header and footer content. If you need to update it, you only need to change it in the template. For example, you can create a header that includes your product's name. If the product name changes, you can change it in the template's header. This approach works fine for headers and footers, but what if you need to include the product name in a paragraph within a topic?

In Flare, you can create variables and snippets to reuse content in multiple topics. Variables and snippets can appear anywhere in a topic, not just in a header or footer.

Variables

A variable can only contain unformatted text. I often use variables for copyright statements and product names. If the copyright statement or the product name changes, I just change my variable's definition and all of my topics are updated.

You can also add system variables to your topics. System variables include the date, time, page count, page number, and topic title.

Variables are stored in a variable set. Flare includes one variable set (named 'Primary') with two variables ('CompanyName' and 'PhoneNumber') when you create or import a project. You can create as many variable sets and variables as you need. Variable sets are stored in a file with a .flvar extension. They appear in the Variables folder in the Project Organizer.

Importing a variable set

If you need to reuse your variables in multiple projects, you can copy a variable set from one project to another. You don't even have to close Flare to import a variable set file.

To import a variable set to your project:

1. In Windows, locate the project that contains the variable set that you want to copy.
2. Open the Project folder.
3. Inside the Project folder, open the VariableSets folder.
4. Copy the variable set file. It will have a .flvar extension.
5. Locate the project to which you want to add the variable set.
6. Open the Project folder.
7. Inside the Project folder, open the VariableSets folder.
8. Paste the variable set file.

Creating a variable set

You can create a new variable set to share variables between projects.

Shortcut	Toolbar	Menu
none	none	Project > Add Variable Set

To create a variable set:

1   Select **Project** > **Add Variable Set**.
    —OR—
    Right-click the Variables folder and select **Add Variable Set**.

    The Add Variable Set dialog box appears.

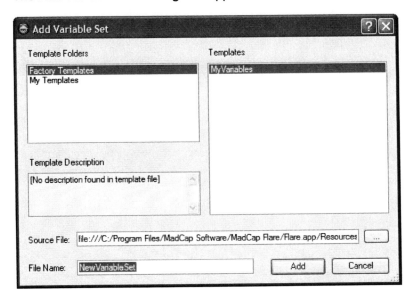

2   Select a **Template Folder** and **Template**.
3   Type a **File Name**.
4   Click **Add**.

To create a variable:

1 Open the **Variables** folder in the Project Organizer.

2 Double-click a variable set.

The Variable Set Editor window appears.

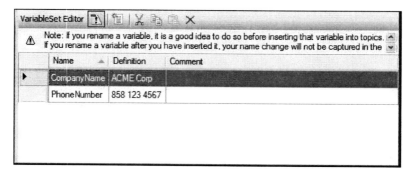

3 Click ![icon] in the Variable Set Editor toolbar.

4 Type a name for the variable.

Be careful naming variables. If you rename a variable after you insert it into your topics, you will have to re-insert the variable into your topics.

5 Type a definition for the variable.

To insert a variable into a topic or master page:

1 Open a topic or master page.

2 Place your cursor where you want to insert the variable.

3 Select **Insert > Insert Variable**.
The Variables dialog box appears.

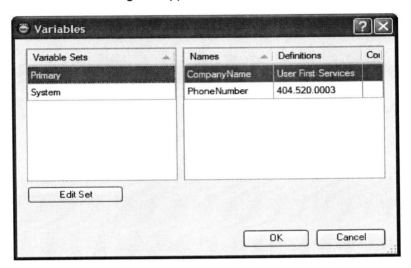

4 Select a variable set.

5 Select a variable.

6 Click **OK**.
The variable appears in the topic.

Variables and snippets | 143

To insert a system variable into a topic or master page:

1 Open a topic or master page.

2 Place your cursor where you want to insert the variable.

3 Select **Insert** > **Insert Variable**.
The Variables dialog box appears.

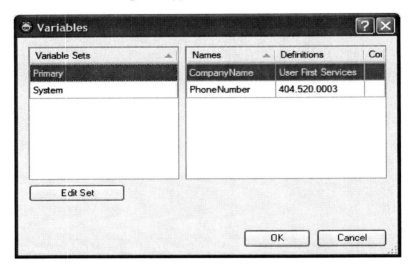

4 Select the **System** variable set.

5 Select a variable.

6 Click **OK**.
The variable appears in the topic.

Snippets NEW!

A snippet can include any type of content, including formatted text, images, and tables. I often create snippets for tables and steps that I need to use in multiple topics.

Snippets are stored in a file with a .flsnp extension. They appear in the Resources\Snippets folder in the Content Explorer.

Creating a snippet using existing content

You can select content within a topic and convert it to a snippet.

Shortcut	Toolbar	Menu
none	none	Format > Create Snippet

To create a snippet using existing content:

1. Open the topic that contains the content that you want to turn into a snippet.

2. Highlight the content that you want to turn into a snippet.

3. Select **Format > Create Snippet**.
   The Create Snippet dialog box appears.

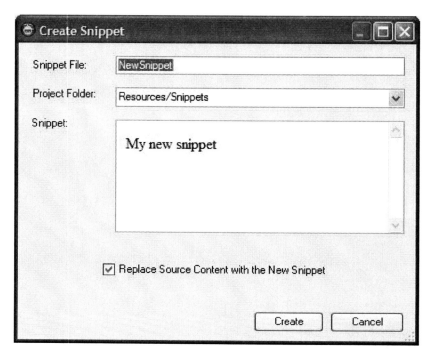

4   In the **Snippet File** field, type a new name for the snippet.

5   Leave the project folder selection as **Resources\Snippets**.

6   If you want the snippet to replace the highlighted text in the topic, select the **Replace Source Content with the New Snippet** option.

7   Click **Create**.
    The snippet is created.

Creating a snippet using new content

You can also create a blank snippet and add content to it.

Shortcut	Toolbar	Menu
none	none	Project > Add Snippet

To create a snippet using new content:

1 Select **Project > Add Snippet**.
  The Add New Snippet dialog box appears.

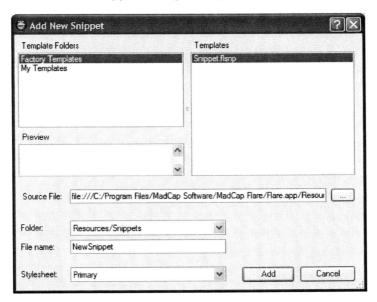

2 Select a **Template Folder** and **Template**.

3 Select a **Folder**.
  By default, snippets are stored in the Resources\Snippets folder.

4 Type a **File Name** for the snippet.

5 Click **Add**.
  The Copy to Project dialog box appears.

Variables and snippets | 147

6   Click **OK**.
    The snippet appears in Content Explorer and opens in the XML Editor.

7   Click inside the snippet page in the XML Editor and add text or other content (such as tables, pictures, and hyperlinks).

Inserting a snippet

You can insert snippets into topics and master pages.

Shortcut	Toolbar	Menu
none	none	Insert > Insert Snippet

To insert a snippet to a topic:

1   Open a topic.

2   Position the cursor where you want to insert the snippet.

3   Select **Insert** > **Insert Snippet**.
    The Insert Snippet Link appears.

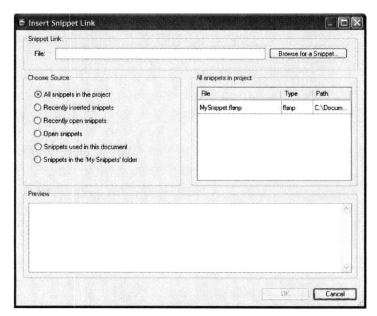

4 Select a snippet **Source**.

5 Select a snippet.
   A preview of the snippet appears.

6 Click **OK**.
   The snippet is added to the topic.

Importing a snippet

If you need to reuse your snippets in multiple projects, you can copy a snippet file from one project to another project. As with variable set and HTML files, you don't have to close Flare to import a snippet file.

To import a snippet:

1 In Windows, locate the project that contains the variable set that you want to copy.

2 Open the Content folder.

3 Inside the Content folder, open the Resources folder, then open the Snippets folder.

4 Copy the snippet file. It will have a .flsnp extension.

5 Locate the project to which you want to insert the snippet file.

6 Open the Content folder.

7 Inside the Content folder, open the Resources folder, then open the Snippets folder.

8 Paste the snippet file.
   The snippet file appears in the Resources\Snippets folder in the Content Explorer.

Variables and snippets | 149

Condition tags

Condition tags can be used to include or exclude content when you create help or printed documentation. For example, you could create an 'External' tag and an 'Internal' tag to produce an external version of your help for customers and an internal version for the technical support department. Or, you could create a 'PrintOnly' tag to only include selected content when you create printed documentation.

In RoboHelp, you can apply a conditional build tag to a topic or content inside of a topic. In Flare, you can apply a condition tag to almost anything: folders, topics, content in topics, TOC entries, index entries, glossary terms, stylesheets, variables, and snippets. Flare also makes it easier to specify which tags you want to include and exclude when you create a target.

In Flare, condition tags are stored in a condition tag set. When you import a RoboHelp project that contains conditional build tags, your tags are stored in a condition tag named 'Primary.' You can add as many condition tag sets and tags as you need.

Conditional tag sets have a .flcts extension. They appear in the Conditional Text folder in the Project Organizer.

'What are those boxes in the Content Explorer?'

They're called 'condition tag boxes.'

When you create a condition tag in RoboHelp or Flare, you assign a color to the tag. This color is used to identify tagged content in a topic. Unlike RoboHelp, Flare can also identify tagged folders and topics. If a folder or topic is associated with a tag, the condition tag box is filled with the tag's assigned color. If the folder or topic is associated with multiple tags, the condition tag box uses vertical stripes to show each tag's color.

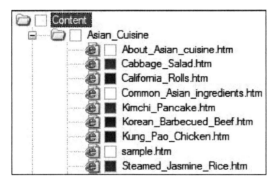

Importing condition tags

If you need to reuse condition tags in multiple projects, you can copy a conditional tag set file from one project to another project.

To import a condition tag set:

1. In Windows, locate the project that contains the condition tag set that you want to copy.
2. Open the Project folder.
3. Inside the Project folder, open the ConditionTagSets folder.
4. Copy the condition tag set file.
   Condition tag set files have a .flcts extension.

5 Locate the project to which you want to import the condition tag set file.

6 Open the Project folder.

7 Inside the Project folder, open the ConditionTagSets folder.

8 Paste the condition tag set file.

Creating a condition tag

To create a condition tag:

1 Open the Project Organizer.

2 Open the **Conditional Text** folder.

3 Double-click a condition tag set.
   The Condition Tag Set Editor appears.

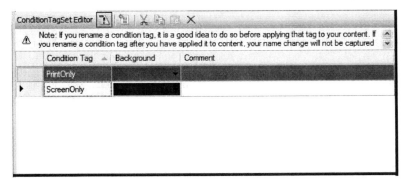

4 Click in the Condition Tag Set Editor toolbar.
   A new tag appears.

5 Double-click the new tag's name.

6 Type a new name for the tag and press **Enter**.

7 Select a color.

   ⚠ *Do not rename a tag after it is applied to topics or content. Flare will not update the tagged content to use the new name, so you will have to reapply the tag to everything.*

Condition tags | 153

Applying a tag to a topic, file, or folder

To apply a tag to a topic, file, or folder:

1 Open the Content Explorer.

2 Select the topic, file, or folder to be tagged.

3 Click ![icon] in the Content Explorer toolbar.
   The Properties dialog box appears.

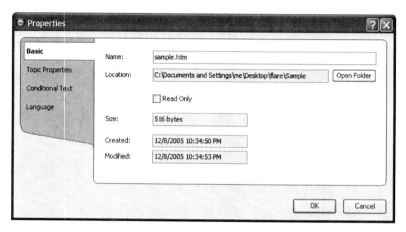

4 Select the **Conditional Text** tab.

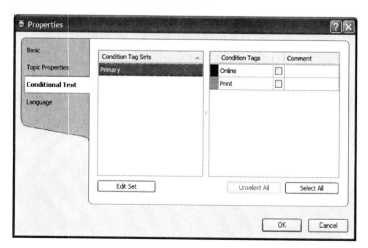

154 | Condition tags

5 Select a tag's checkbox.

6 Click **OK**.

The tag is applied and the file or folder's condition tag box is filled with the tag's color.

Applying a tag to content in a topic

To apply a tag to content in a topic:

1 Open a topic.

2 Select the content to be tagged.
You can apply a tag to any content, including characters, words, paragraphs, table columns/rows, and images.

3 Select **Format** > **Conditions**.
The Condition Tags dialog box appears.

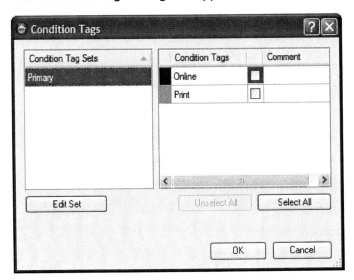

4 Select a condition tag's checkbox.

5 Click **OK**.
The tag is applied. The tagged content is shaded using the tag's color.

Condition tags | 155

Applying a tag to a TOC book or page NEW!

To apply a tag to a TOC book or page:

1 Open the Project Organizer.

2 Double-click a TOC.

3 Select a book or page and click in the TOC Editor. The Properties dialog box appears.

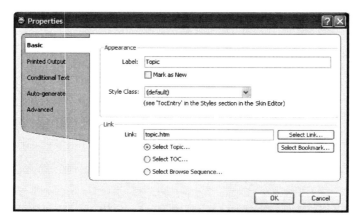

4 Select the **Conditional Text** tab.

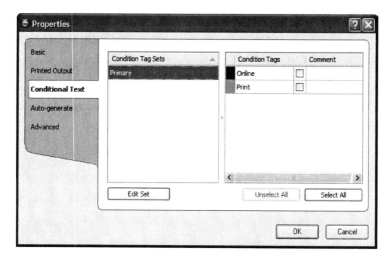

5 Select a tag's checkbox.

6 Click **OK**.
The tag is applied and the Toc book or page's condition tag box is filled with the tag's color.

Applying a tag to an index entry NEW!

To apply a tag to an index entry:

1 Open a topic.

2 Select an index entry marker.

3 Select **Format** > **Conditions**.
The Condition Tags dialog box appears.

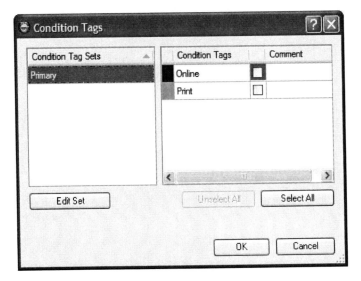

4 Select a condition tag's checkbox.

5 Click **OK**.
The tag is applied. A condition tag box appears inside the tagged index entry's marker.

Targets

RoboHelp and Flare can be used to create several types of online help and printed documentation, as summarized in the following table. In RoboHelp, these output formats are called 'Single Source Layouts.' In Flare, they're called 'Targets.'

RoboHelp is not a 'better' application than Flare just because it creates more types of help. If you need to use a format that Flare does not create, then you should continue to use RoboHelp. However, if you need to create a format that Flare *does* create, like WebHelp, you should compare RoboHelp's output to Flare's output and decide which one works best for your needs.

Target	RoboHelp	Flare
DotNet Help		✓
FlashHelp	✓	
HTML Help	✓	✓
JavaHelp	✓	
Oracle Help	✓	
Printed documentation (Word)	✓	✓
WebHelp	✓	✓
WebHelp Pro	✓*	

* *RoboHelp Office Pro only*

'What is DotNet Help?' NEW!

MadCap's DotNet Help is a new format that was designed to be used with .NET applications. It is similar to WebHelp, but it runs inside the freely distributable Flare Help viewer. Unlike HTML Help and WebHelp, DotNet Help can run from a file server.

HTML Help cannot run from a file server because Microsoft has disabled them for security reasons.

WebHelp (created with RoboHelp or Flare) cannot run from a file server in Internet Explorer using Windows XP SP2 because Microsoft blocks 'active content.' You can enable it, but you have to do it manually and tell your users how to do it.

TIP To enable active content in Internet Explorer, open Internet Explorer, select Tools > Options, click Advanced, and turn on 'Allow active content to run in files on My Computer.'

'What about FlashHelp?'

As you can see in the table on page 159, Flare v1.0 does not create a Flash-based help format like RoboHelp's FlashHelp. According to MadCap Software, a Flash-based format was not included because the Flash player has trouble reflowing text when you resize the window. MadCap Software has stated that they will add a Flash-based help format to Flare as soon as the Flash player is updated.

'Is Flare's WebHelp the same as RoboHelp's WebHelp?'

Flare's version of WebHelp looks very different from RoboHelp's WebHelp. Flare's WebHelp uses an accordion structure, like Flare itself, to display the TOC, index, search, and glossary. Flare's WebHelp also has some new options, such as the ability to highlight the user's search term in a topic.

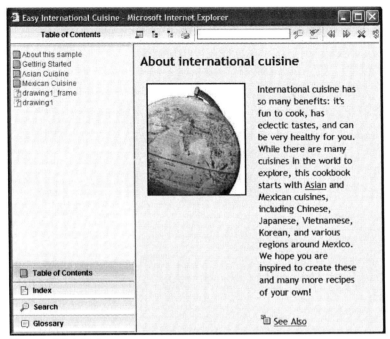

Flare's WebHelp

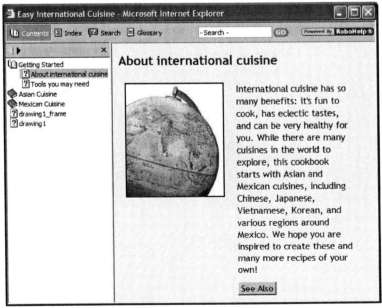

RoboHelp's WebHelp

Creating a target

You should create a different target for each version of your online help or printed documentation. For example, if you need to create WebHelp and printed documentation for the 'Standard' and 'Professional' versions of your product, you should create four targets.

Shortcut	Toolbar	Menu
none	none	Project > Add Target

To create a target:

1 Select **Project > Add Target**.
—OR—
Right-click the Targets folder and select **Add Target**.

The Add New Item dialog box appears.

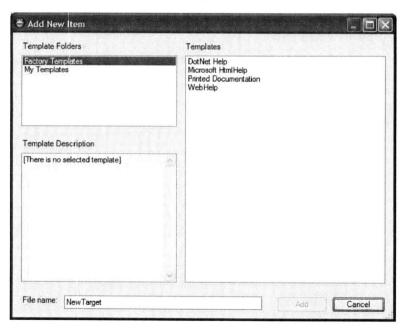

2 Select a **Template Folder** and **Template**.

3 Type a **File Name**.
   You don't have to type the .fltar extension. Flare will add it for you if you leave it out.

4 Click **Add**.
   The target appears in the Targets folder in the Project Organizer and opens in the Target Editor.

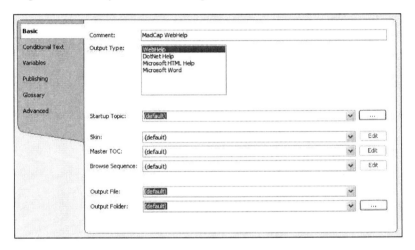

5 Click **Save**.

Setting up a help target

You can create a help target to specify the skin, master page, TOC, condition tags, variables, and glossaries that are used in your help system.

To set up a help target:

1 Open the target.

2 On the Basic tab, select the following options:

   ▫ **Comment** — a short description of the target.

   ▫ **Output Type** — the help format that you are creating.

   ▫ **Startup Topic** — the first topic that appears when the user opens your help system.

Targets | 163

- **Skin** — the skin file specifies the size, appearance, and features included in a target.
- **Master TOC** — the TOC that will be used for the target.
- **Browse Sequence** — the browse sequence that will be used for the target.
- **Output File** — the name of the main entry file for your help system.
- **Output Folder** — where the generated help files will be created.

3 Select the **Conditional Text** tab.

4 Select whether you want to include or exclude each tag.

5 Select the **Variables** tab.

6 If you need to change a variable's definition for the target, click inside its Definition cell and type a new value.

7 If you want to publish your online help to a file or web server:
- Select the **Publishing** tab.
- Select a destination.
  —OR—
  Click **New Destination** to create a publishing destination.

8 Select the **Glossary** tab and select the following options:
- **Glossary Term Conversion** method — how your glossary terms are converted in your topics.
- **Glossary** — the glossary (or glossaries) that are included in your target.

9 Select the **Advanced** tab and select the following options:
- **Stylesheet Medium** — if your stylesheet contains a medium, you can use the medium's styles or the stylesheet's default styles.
- **Search Filter** — users can use search filters to search within a group a topics.

- **Alias File** — if you are creating context-sensitive help, the alias file matches help topics to application windows and dialog boxes.

10 Click **Save**.

Setting up a printed documentation target

You can create a printed documentation target to specify the condition tags, variables, and glossaries that are used in your printed documentation.

To set up a printed documentation target:

1 Open the target.

2 On the Basic tab, select the following options:

- **Comment** — a short description of the target.

- **Output Type** — the help format that you are creating.

- **Master TOC** — the TOC that will be used for the target.

- **Output Folder** — where the generated files will be created.

3 Select the **Conditional Text** tab.

4 Select whether you want to include or exclude each tag.

5 Select the **Variables** tab.

6 If you need to change a variable's definition for the target, click inside its Definition cell and type a new value.

7 If you want to publish your printed documentation to a file or web server:

- Select the **Publishing** tab.

- Select a destination.
  —OR—
  Click **New Destination** to create a publishing destination.

8 Select the **Glossary** tab.

9 Select a **Glossary** (or glossaries) to include in your documentation.

10 Select the **Advanced** tab.

11 If your stylesheet contains a medium, select whether you want to use the medium's styles instead of the stylesheet's default styles.

12 Click **Save**.

Building a target

RoboHelp's default folder for generated layouts is named '!SSL!' In Flare, the default folder is named 'Outputs.' You can change the default folder in RoboHelp or Flare, but most users use these default folders.

Shortcut	Toolbar	Menu
F6		Build > Build Primary

To build a target:

1 Click the down arrow beside the icon and select a target.
—OR—
Right-click a target and select **Build**.

2 If you made any changes to the target, Flare will prompt you to save your changes. Click **Yes**.
The Build Progress dialog box appears.

3 When the build is complete, click **Yes** to view the generated target.

Building a target from the command line

Flare targets can be compiled from the command line. This feature can be used to build your targets when you compile an application.

To build a target from the command line:

1 Open a command prompt.

2 Navigate to the directory where you installed Flare.
The default directory is program files\madcap software\madcap flare\flare.app.

3 Type **madbuild -project <path><projectfilename>**.
For example: madbuild - project c:\myFolder\myProject.flprj.

To build all of your targets from the command line:

1 Open a command prompt.

2 Navigate to the directory where you installed Flare.
The default directory is program files\madcap software\madcap flare\flare.app.

3 Type **madbuild -project <path><projectname> -target <targetname>**.
For example:
madbuild - project c:\myFolder\myProject.flprj -target myWebHelp.

Viewing a target

- Click the 👓 icon's arrow and select a target.
  —OR—
  Right-click a target and select **View**.

Publishing a target

You can publish any target to a file server or an FTP server. Like RoboHelp, Flare allows you to publish to multiple publishing destinations at the same time.

Shortcut	Toolbar	Menu
Ctrl+F6		Build > Publish Primary

To create a publishing destination:

1 Open a WebHelp target.

2 Select the **Publishing** tab.

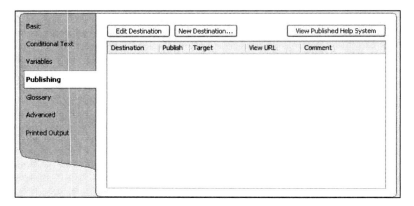

3 Click **New Destination**.

The Add New Item dialog box appears.

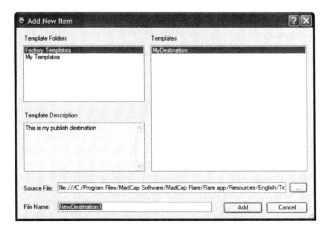

4   Select a **Template Folder** and **Template**.

5   Type a **File Name**.

6   Click **Add**.
    The destination appears in the Destinations folder in the Project Organizer and opens in the Destination Editor.

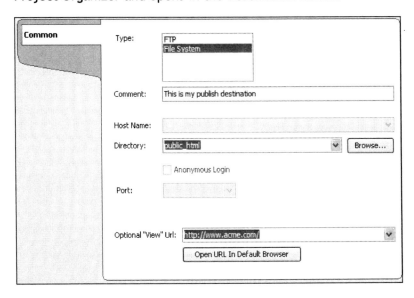

7   Select a destination type.

Targets | 169

8 Type a **Comment**.

9 Click **Browse** to select a publishing directory.

10 Click **Save**.

To publish a target:

1 Open a target.

2 Click .

The Publishing Target dialog box appears.

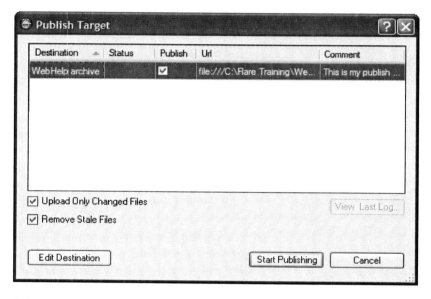

3 Select one (or more) of the publishing destinations.

4 Select **Upload Only Changed Files** to only republished files that have changed.

5 Select **Remove Stale Files** to remove files from the server that have been removed from your project.

6 Click **Start Publishing**.
Flare copies the generated files to the publishing destination.

Context-sensitive help

Context-sensitive help (or 'CSH' if you like acronyms) is help that opens to a specific topic based on where you are in an application. For example, a 'Print Preview' dialog box would open a help topic about printing, and a 'Save' dialog box would open a topic about saving a file. RoboHelp and Flare both provide context-sensitive help. They also provide built-in tools to help you link your help to a software application.

To create context-sensitive help, you need to associate your help topics to the windows and dialog boxes that are used in your application. This process is called 'mapping,' and it uses two files: header files and alias files.

Adding a header file

A header file is used to assign a number and an ID to each dialog box and window in an application. Many programming applications create header files automatically, but you can also create header files using Flare. Header files have a .h or .hh extension, and they appear in the Advanced folder in the Project Organizer.

Header files use the following format:
`#define MyID number`

For example:
`#define Save_dialog 1000`

Shortcut	Toolbar	Menu
none	none	Project > Advanced > Add Header File

To create a header file:

If your software team has created a header file, you can copy it to the Advanced folder in the Project folder. If you need to create a header file, follow these steps.

1   Select **Project > Advanced > Add Header File**.

    The Add Header File dialog box appears.

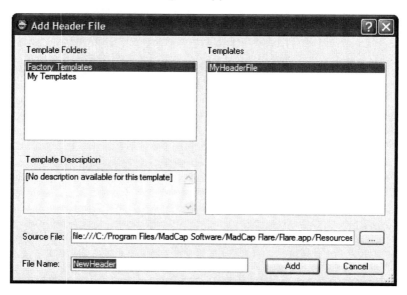

2   Select a **Template Folder** and **Template**.

3   Type a **File Name** for the header file.
    You don't have to type the .h extension. Flare will add it for you if you leave it out.

4   Click **Add**.
    The header file appears in the Advanced folder in the Project Organizer and opens in the Text Editor.

Creating an alias file

Alias files are used to match IDs to a help topic. At first, an alias file might seem unnecessary: why not just put everything in the header file? The reason is that you need to share the header file with the development team. They usually need it to compile the application, and their programming application might automatically update the header file. By using an alias file, you can keep linking topics to IDs while the developers are creating the application.

In Flare, alias files can also be used to assign a skin to a help topic when it is opened from the application. For example, you could normally open your help system in a large, 700x500 window with the navigation pane on the left. When you open it from a context-sensitive link, it could open in a smaller window without the navigation pane.

Alias files have an .flali extension. They appear in the Project Organizer in the Advanced folder.

Shortcut	Toolbar	Menu
none	none	Project > Advanced > Add Alias File

To create an alias file:

1 Select **Project>Advanced>Add Alias File**.
   The Add Alias File dialog box appears.

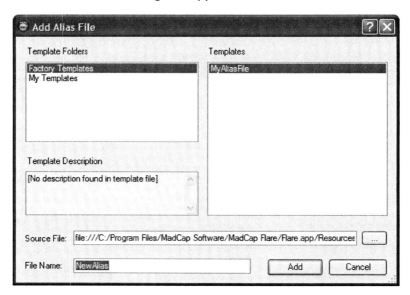

2 Select a **Template Folder** and **Template**.

3 Type a **File Name** for the alias file.
   You don't have to type the .flali extension. Flare will add it for you if you leave it out.

4 Click **Add**.
   The alias file appears in the Advanced folder in the Project Organizer and opens in the Alias Editor.

To assign an ID to a topic:

1 Open the alias file.
   Alias files are stored in the Advanced folder in the Project Organizer.

2 On the left side of the Alias Editor, select an ID.

3   On the right side of the Alias Editor, select a topic to link to the ID.

4   If you want to use a skin when opening the topic, select the skin.

5   Click **Assign**.
    The topic's filename appears in the **Topic** column.

6   Continue assigning topics to IDs.

7   Save your alias file.
    You can open your alias file and add new IDs at any time.

Testing context-sensitive help

After you assign IDs to your topics, you can test your context-sensitive help links. You can test context-sensitive HTML Help and WebHelp.

To test your context-sensitive help:

1   Build your target.

2   Right-click your target and select **Test CSH API Calls**.
    The Context-sensitive Help API Tester dialog box appears.

3   Next to each identifier, click [Test].
    The correct help topic should appear.

4   When you are finished testing, click **Close**.

Keyboard shortcuts (by task)

Opening projects and topics

Shortcut	Description
F4	Open the Properties dialog box from the Content Explorer
Ctrl+O	Open a project
Ctrl+T	Create a new topic
Ctrl+Shift+P	Open the Properties dialog box from within the XML Editor

Selecting text

Shortcut	Description
Ctrl+Left Arrow	Move the cursor to the next word to the left
Ctrl+Right Arrow	Move the cursor to the next word to the right
Ctrl+Shift+Left Arrow	Select the next word to the left
Ctrl+Shift+Right Arrow	Select the next word to the right
Ctrl+A	Select all
Ctrl+C	Copy
Ctrl+V	Paste
Ctrl+Z	Undo
Del	Delete
Shift+Tab	Select the previous cell in a table
Tab	Select the next cell in a table, or when you press Tab in the last row of a table, add a new row

Formatting text

Shortcut	Description
F12	Open the Style window
Ctrl+F12	Open the Local Formatting window
Ctrl+Alt+B	Open the Paragraph Properties dialog box
Ctrl+Shift+B	Open the Font Properties dialog box
Shift+F12	Open the Attributes window
Ctrl+B	Bold
Ctrl+I	Italic
Ctrl+U	Underline
Ctrl+X	Cut
Ctrl+Y	Redo

Linking

Shortcut	Description
Ctrl+K	Insert a hyperlink
Ctrl+Shift+K	Insert a bookmark
Ctrl+Shift+R	Insert a cross reference
Ctrl+Shift+T	Insert a glossary term link
Shift+F9	Open the Concept Entry window

Saving

Shortcut	Description
Ctrl+S	Save
Alt+Ctrl+S	Save as
Ctrl+Shift+S	Save all

Spell checking

Shortcut	Description
F7	Open the Spell Check window

Working with the index and TOC

Shortcut	Description
F2	Highlight TOC entry for editing
F9	Open the Index Entry window
F10	Insert the selected text as an index keyword
Ctrl+F8	Open the 'master' TOC

Searching

Shortcut	Description
F3	Find next
Alt+Ctrl+F	Open the Find in Files window
Ctrl+F	Open the Find and Replace window
Ctrl+Shift+F	Add the selected text to the 'Find what' field in the Find and Replace or Find in Files window

Opening and docking windows

Shortcut	Description
Ctrl+J	Open the Content Explorer
Ctrl+W	Open the Project Organizer
Ctrl+Shift+D	Move the active document to the Document Dock
Ctrl+Shift+W	Open the Start page

Publishing

Shortcut	Description
F6	Build the primary target
Ctrl+F6	Publish the primary target
Shift+F6	Open the primary target

Opening Flare's help system

Shortcut	Description
F1	Open a context-sensitive help topic
Alt-Ctrl+F1	Open the help system's TOC
Alt+F1	Open the help system's index
Alt+Shift+F2	Open the help system's index results window
Ctrl+F1	Open the help system's search
Ctrl+F3	Open a context-sensitive help topic in the dynamic help window

Keyboard shortcuts (by key)

Shortcut	Description
Alt+Ctrl+B	Open the Paragraph Properties dialog box
Alt+Ctrl+F	Open the Find in Files window
Alt+Ctrl+S	Save as
Alt-Ctrl+F1	Open the Flare help system's TOC
Alt+Shift+F2	Open the Flare help system's index results window
Alt+F1	Open the Flare help system's index
Ctrl+F1	Open the Flare help system's search
Ctrl+F3	Open a context-sensitive help topic in the dynamic help window
Ctrl+F6	Publish the primary target
Ctrl+F8	Open the 'master' TOC
Ctrl+F12	Open the Local Formatting window
Ctrl+A	Select all
Ctrl+B	Bold
Ctrl+C	Copy
Ctrl+F	Open the Find and Replace window
Ctrl+I	Italic
Ctrl+J	Opens the Content Explorer
Ctrl+K	Insert a hyperlink
Ctrl+O	Open a new project
Ctrl+P	Print
Ctrl+S	Save
Ctrl+T	Create a new topic
Ctrl+U	Underline

Shortcut	Description
Ctrl+V	Paste
Ctrl+W	Open the Project Organizer
Ctrl+X	Cut
Ctrl+Y	Redo
Ctrl+Z	Undo
Ctrl+Left Arrow	Move the insertion point cursor to the next word to the left
Ctrl+Right Arrow	Move the insertion point cursor to the next word to the right
Ctrl+Shift+B	Open the Font Properties dialog box
Ctrl+Shift+D	Move the active document to the Document Dock
Ctrl+Shift+F	Add the selected text to the 'Find what' field in the Find and Replace or Find in Files window
Ctrl+Shift+K	Insert a bookmark
Ctrl+Shift+P	Open the Properties dialog box from within the XML Editor
Ctrl+Shift+R	Insert a cross reference
Ctrl+Shift+S	Save all
Ctrl+Shift+T	Insert a glossary term link
Ctrl+Shift+W	Open the Start page
Ctrl+Shift+Left Arrow	Select the next word to the left
Ctrl+Shift+Right Arrow	Select the next word to the right
Del	Delete
F1	Open a context-sensitive help topic
F2	Highlight for editing
F3	Find next
F4	Open the Properties dialog box from the Content Explorer

Shortcut	Description
F6	Build the primary target
F7	Open the Spell Check window
F9	Open the Index Entry window
F10	Insert the selected text as an index keyword
F12	Open the Style window
Shift+F6	Open the primary target
Shift+F9	Open the Concept Entry window
Shift+F12	Open the Attributes window
Shift+Tab	Select the previous cell in a table
Tab	Select the next cell in a table, or, if you press Tab in the last row of a table, add a new row

Toolbar comparison

The table below compares RoboHelp's toolbars to Flare's global and local toolbars.

RoboHelp's Project toolbar

Button Description	RoboHelp	Flare
Save		
Build Primary Target		
View Primary Target		
Publish Primary Target	File > Batch Generate	
Open Primary Target	--	
Create New Topic		
Spell Check		F7
Print		--
Edit		
Properties		
Cut		
Copy		

Button Description	RoboHelp	Flare
Paste	📋	📋
Delete	✗	✗
Preview Topic	👓	📄 (in the XML Editor)
Undo	↶	↶ Undo Enter ▼
Redo	↷	↷ Redo Typing ▼

RoboHelp's Objects toolbar

Button Description	RoboHelp	Flare
Insert Hyperlink	🔗	🔗 (in the XML Editor)
Insert Popup	💬	🔗 (in the XML Editor)
Insert Bookmark	🔖	Ctrl+Shift+K
Insert Navigation Control	🎯	Insert > Drop-down Text Insert > Toggler Insert > Expanding Text
Insert RoboDemo Movie	▶	🖼 (in the XML Editor)
Insert Picture	🖼	🖼 (in the XML Editor)
Create Rectangular Image Map Shape	☐	📐 (in the Image Map Editor)

Button Description	RoboHelp	Flare
Create Oval Image Map Shape	○	(in the Image Map Editor)
Create Polygon Image Map Shape	⬠	(in the Image Map Editor)

RoboHelp's Formatting toolbar

Button Description	RoboHelp	Flare
Assign Stylesheet		Tools > Stylesheet Links
Change Font Color	A	A ▾
Change Underline Color		
Apply Bold	**B**	**B**
Apply Italic	*I*	*I*
Apply Underline	U	U
Superscript	Format > Font	x^2
Subscript	Format > Font	x_2
Font Properties	Format > Font	A
Unformat	--	
Align Left		

Button Description	RoboHelp	Flare
Align Center		
Align Right		
Justify		
Numbered List		
Bulleted List		
Decrease Indent		
Increase Indent		
List Actions (merge and sort)	N/A	
Show/Hide Paragraphs	¶	¶ (in the XML Editor)

Guide to Flare files

The following table lists all of the file types that are used in Flare, their extension, and their default folder.

File Type	Extension	Default Folder
Browse sequence	flbrs	Project\Advanced
Condition tag set	flcts	Project\ConditionTagSets
Context-sensitive help alias file	flali	Project\Advanced
Context-sensitive help header file	h or hh	Project\Advanced
Dictionary	tlx	Program Files\MadCap Software\MadCap Flare\Flare.app\Resources\SSCE
DotNet Help startup topic	mchelp	Output*name of DotNet Help target*
Flash movie	swf	Content
Glossary	flglo	Project\Glossaries
HTML Help	chm	Output*name of HTML Help target*
Image	bmp, gif, jpg, png, tif	New projects: Content\Resources\Images Imported projects: Content
Master page	flmsp	Content\Resources\MasterPages
Project file	flprj	top-level folder
Publishing destination	fldes	Project\Destinations
Search filter set	flsfs	Project\Advanced
Skin	flskn	Project\Skins
Snippet	flsnp	Content\Resources\Snippets

File Type	Extension	Default Folder
Stylesheet	css	New projects: Content\Resources\Stylesheets Imported projects: Content (for imported projects)
Table stylesheet	css	Content\Resources\TableStyles
Target	fltar	Project\Targets
Target Build Error Log	mclog	Project\Reports
TOC	fltoc	Project\TOCs
Topic (generated)	htm	Output
Topic (source)	htm	Content
Variable set	flvar	Project\VariableSets
Window layout	panellayout	Documents and Settings\me\Application Data\MadCap Software
Word import template	flimp	Project\Imports

'What about all those other RoboHelp files?'

RoboHelp uses multiple .apj and .fpj files to track your project. Flare doesn't need to use these files, so you won't see them in your Flare folder when you import a project. The information is still a part of your project, but you don't have to deal with these 'extra' files when you use Flare.

Quick task index

The quick task index provides the basic steps for every major task you can perform in Flare.

Concept	See Page
Projects	194
Topics	195
Topic content	196
Links	197
Navigational tools	200
Formatting	201
Variables and snippets	202
Condition tags	203
Targets	204
Context-sensitive help	205

Projects

Task	Steps		See Page
Creating a project	1	Select **File > New Project**.	28
	2	Type a **Project Name** and **Project Folder** and click **Next**.	
	3	Select a **Language** and click **Next**.	
	4	Select a **Template Folder** and **Template** and click **Next**.	
	5	Select an **Available Target** and click **Next**.	
	6	Select **Create the Project** and click **Finish**.	
Creating a project based on a Word document	1	Select **File > Import Project > Import Word Documents**.	57
	2	Click **Next**.	
	3	Click **Add Files**, select a file, and click **Open**.	
	4	Select whether you want to link to the original Word document and click **Next**.	
	5	Type a **Project Name**, type or select a **Project Folder**, and click **Next**.	
	6	Select a style or styles to use to create new topics and click **Next**.	
	7	Select whether you want to create new topics based on the length of your Word document and click **Next**.	
	8	Select a stylesheet and click **Next**.	
	9	Map your styles and click **Next**.	
	10	Click **Finish**.	
Importing a project	1	Select **File > Import Project > Import (Non-Flare) Project**.	30
	2	Click ▭ to find the project.	
	3	Locate and select a project to import.	
	4	Click **Open**.	
	5	Type a **Project Name** and select a **Project Folder**.	
	6	Select whether you want to **Convert all topics at once** and/or to **Convert inline formatting to CSS styles**.	
	7	Click **Finish**.	

Topics

Task	Steps		See Page
Creating a topic	1	Select **Project** > **Add Topic**.	37
	2	Select a **Template Folder** and **Template**.	
	3	Type a **File Name**.	
	4	Select a **Stylesheet**.	
	5	Click **Add** and click **OK**.	
Importing a Word document	1	Create or open an MS Word import file.	57
	2	Click **Add Files**.	
	3	Select a Word document and click **Open**.	
	4	Select whether you want to link the generated files to the source files.	
	5	Select the **New Topic Styles** tab and select the styles to use to create new topics.	
	6	Select the **Options** tab and select whether you want to create new topics based on the length of your Word document.	
	7	Select the **Stylesheet** tab and select a stylesheet.	
	8	Select the **Paragraph Styles** tab and map your paragraph styles.	
	9	Select the **Character Styles** tab and map your character styles.	
	10	Click **Import** and click **Accept**.	
Importing an HTML file	1	In Windows Explorer, find the HTML file (or files) you want to import.	63
	2	Copy the file(s) to your project's Content folder.	

Topic content

Task	Steps	See Page
Creating a list	1 Click the down arrow to the right of the ☰ icon in the Text format toolbar. 2 Select a list type. 3 Type the list items.	45
Sorting a list	1 Select the list. 2 Click ☰ to view the block bars. 3 Click the list's ol or ul tag. 4 Select **Sort List**.	46
Inserting a table	1 Select **Table > Insert > Table**. 2 Select a number of columns and rows. 3 Select a number of header and footer rows. 4 Type a table caption and select a caption location. 5 Select a column width. 6 Click **OK**.	47
Creating a table style	1 Select **Project > Add Table Style**. 2 Select a **Template Folder** and **Template**. 3 Select a **Folder**. 4 Type a **File Name**. 5 Click **Add** and click **OK**.	50
Assigning a table style to a table	1 Click inside a table. 2 Select **Table > Table Properties**. 3 Select a **Table Style**. 4 Click **OK**.	55
Inserting an image or video	1 Select **Insert > Insert Picture**. 2 Click **Browse for a file**, select an image file, and click **Open**. 3 Type a **Screen Tip**. 4 Click **OK**.	65

Links

Task	Steps		See Page
Creating a link	1	Select the text or image that you want to use as the link.	69
	2	Select **Insert** > **Insert Hyperlink**.	
	3	Select the type of link you want to create.	
	4	Select a link target (a topic, file, or website).	
	5	Select a **Target Frame**.	
	6	Type a **Screen Tip**.	
	7	Click **OK**.	
Creating an image map link	1	Select the image to which you want to add links and select **Image Map**.	74
	2	Select an image map shape and draw the image map area.	
	3	Select a link target type and target.	
	4	Select a **Target Frame**.	
	5	Type a **Screen Tip**.	
	6	Click **OK**.	
Creating a topic popup	1	Select the text or image that you want to use as the link.	75
	2	Select **Insert** > **Insert Topic Popup**.	
	3	Select the type of link you want to create.	
	4	Select a link target (a topic, file, or website).	
	5	Select **Popup Window** as the **Target Frame**.	
	6	Type a **Screen Tip**.	
	7	Click **OK**.	
Creating a text popup	1	Select the text or image that you want to use as the link.	77
	2	Select **Insert** > **Insert Popup**.	
	3	Type the popup text.	
	4	Click **OK**.	

Drop-down, expanding, and toggler links

Task	Steps		See Page
Creating a drop-down link	1	Open the topic that will contain the drop-down link.	80
	2	Highlight the drop-down link and drop-down text.	
	3	Select **Insert > Insert Drop-Down Text**.	
	4	Highlight the drop-down link (or "head").	
	5	Click **OK**.	
Creating an expanding link	1	Open the topic that will contain the expanding link.	81
	2	Highlight the expanding link and expanding text.	
	3	Select **Insert > Insert Expanding Text**.	
	4	Highlight the expanding link (or "hotspot").	
	5	Click **OK**.	
Creating a toggler link	1	Click the tag bar next to the content that you want to toggle.	82
	2	In the popup menu, select **Name**.	
	3	Type a name for the toggled element and click **OK**.	
	4	Highlight the text that you want to use as the toggler hotspot.	
	5	Select **Insert > Insert Toggler**.	
	6	Select a toggler target.	
	7	Click **OK**.	

Related topic, keyword, and concept links

Task	Steps		See Page
Creating a related topics link	1	Select **Insert** > **Insert Help Control** > **Related Topics Control**.	86
	2	Select a topic to add to the link.	
	3	Click [<<<] to add the topic to the related topics link.	
	4	Add more topics as needed.	
	5	Click **OK**.	
Creating a keyword link	1	Select **Insert** > **Insert Help Control** > **Keyword Link Control**.	87
	2	Select a keyword.	
	3	Click [<<<] to add the keyword to the keyword link.	
	4	Add more keywords as needed.	
	5	Click **OK**.	
Creating a concept link	1	Add a concept group.	88
	2	Open a topic to associate with the concept group.	
	3	Select **Tools** > **Concepts** > **Concept Entry Window**.	
	4	Type a term and press **Enter**.	
	5	Click **Save**.	
	6	Select **Insert** > **Insert Help Control** > **Concept Link**.	
	7	Select a concept.	
	8	Click [<<<] to add the concept to the concept link.	
	9	Click **OK**.	

Quick task index | **199**

Navigational tools

Task	Steps		See Page
Creating a browse sequence	1	Select **Project** > **Advanced** > **Add Browse Sequence**.	91
	2	Select a **Template Folder** and **Template**.	
	3	Type a **File Name**.	
	4	Click **Add** and Click **OK**.	
Creating a TOC book	1	Click .	100
	2	Click in the TOC Editor toolbar.	
	3	Press **F2**.	
	4	Type a name.	
Creating a TOC page	1	Click .	100
	2	Double-click the TOC page.	
	3	Type a **Label** for the page.	
	4	Click **Select Link**.	
	5	Select a topic.	
	6	Click **Open**.	
	7	Click **OK**.	
Creating an index entry	1	Click before or on the word or phrase that you want to insert as an index entry.	108
	2	Press **F9**.	
	3	Type a term and press **Enter**.	
Creating a glossary entry and link	1	Highlight the word or phrase that will become the glossary link.	113
	2	Select **Insert** > **Insert Glossary Term Link**.	
	3	Select a **Glossary File**.	
	4	Type a definition.	
	5	Click **OK**.	

Formatting

Task	Steps		See Page
Creating a stylesheet	1	Select **Project > Add Stylesheet**.	122
	2	Select a **Template Folder** and **Template**.	
	3	Select a **Folder**.	
	4	Type a **File Name**.	
	5	Click **Add**.	
	6	Click **OK**.	
Creating a style	1	Use the **Format** menu commands to format the text.	124
	2	Click inside the formatted content. Do not highlight the content.	
	3	Select **View > Style Window**.	
	4	Click **Create Style**.	
	5	Type a name for the new style.	
	6	Select whether the style should be applied to the highlighted content.	
	7	Click **OK**.	
Creating a master page	1	Select **Project > Add Master Page**.	132
	2	Select a template folder and template.	
	3	Type a file name for the master page.	
	4	Select a stylesheet.	
	5	Click **Add**.	
	6	Click **OK**.	
Creating a skin	1	Select **Project > Add Skin**.	135
	2	Select a template folder and template.	
	3	Type a file name for the skin.	
	4	Click **Add**.	
	5	Modify the skin options as needed.	

Variables and snippets

Task	Steps		See Page
Creating a variable	1	Click in the Variable Set Editor toolbar.	142
	2	Type a name for the variable.	
	3	Type a definition for the variable.	
Inserting a variable	1	Select **Insert > Insert Variable**.	143
	2	Select a variable set.	
	3	Select a variable.	
	4	Click **OK**.	
Creating a snippet from existing content	1	Highlight the content you want to convert to a snippet.	145
	2	Select **Format > Create Snippet**.	
	3	Type a name for the snippet.	
	4	Select **Replace Source Content with the New Snippet**.	
	5	Click **Create**.	
Creating a snippet from new content	1	Select **Project > Add Snippet**.	147
	2	Select a **Template Folder** and **Template**.	
	3	Type a **File Name**.	
	4	Click **Add**.	
	5	Click **OK**.	
Inserting a snippet	1	Select **Insert > Insert Snippet**.	148
	2	Select a **Snippet Source**.	
	3	Select a snippet.	
	4	Click **OK**.	

Condition tags

Task	Steps	See Page
Creating a condition tag	1 Open a condition tag set. 2 Click in the Condition Tag Set Editor toolbar. 3 Press **F2**. 4 Type a new name for the tag and press **Enter**. 5 Select a color.	153
Applying a condition tag to a topic, file, or folder	1 Select the topic, file, or folder to be tagged. 2 Click in the Content Explorer toolbar. 3 Select the **Conditional Text** tab. 4 Select a tag's checkbox. 5 Click **OK**.	154
Applying a condition tag to content	1 Select the content to be tagged. 2 Select **Format > Conditions**. 3 Select a condition tag's checkbox. 4 Click **OK**.	155
Applying a condition tag to a TOC book or page	1 Open the TOC. 2 Select a book or page and click . 3 Select the **Conditional Text** tab. 4 Select a tag's checkbox. 5 Click **OK**.	156

Targets

Task	Steps		See Page
Creating a target	1	Select Project > **Add Target**.	162
	2	Select a template folder and template.	
	3	Type a file name.	
	4	Click **Add**.	
	5	Click **Save**.	
	6	Set the target options as needed.	
Building a target	▫	Right-click a target and select **Build**.	166
Viewing a target	▫	Right-click a target and select **View**.	167
Creating a publishing destination	1	Open a target.	168
	2	Select Project > **Add Destination**.	
	3	Select a template folder and template.	
	4	Type a file name.	
	5	Click **Add**.	
	6	Select a target type.	
	7	Type a **comment**.	
	8	Select a publishing location.	
Publishing a target	1	Open a target.	168
	2	Click ▣.	
	3	Select one (or more) of the publishing destinations.	
	4	Click **Start Publishing**.	

Context-sensitive help

Task	Steps	See Page
Creating a header file	1 Select **Project > Advanced > Add Header File**. 2 Select a **Template Folder** and **Template**. 3 Type a **File Name**. 4 Click **Add**.	173
Creating an alias file	1 Select **Project > Advanced > Add Alias File**. 2 Select a **Template Folder** and **Template**. 3 Type a **File Name**. 4 Click **Add**.	173
Assigning an ID to a topic	1 Open an alias file. 2 Select an **ID**. 3 Select a **Topic**. 4 Select a **Skin** (optional). 5 Click **Assign**.	174
Testing context-sensitive help	1 Build your target. 2 Right-click the target in the Targets folder and select **Test CSH API Calls**. 3 Next to each identifier, click **Test**.	175

Index

Acrobat
    announced support for, 19
ActiveX.dll
    why it's not needed, 97, 119
Alias files
    creating, 173, 205
APJ files
    why Flare doesn't use them, 192
Brazilian Portuguese
    suport for, 27
Breadcrumbs proxy, 133
Browse sequences
    associating with a target, 96
    creating, 91, 95, 200
    creating based on a TOC, 95
    enabling in a skin, 96
    viewing in help systems, 21
    viewing in help systems, 97
Building targets
    DotNet Help, 166, 167, 204
    HTML Help, 166, 167, 204
    printed documentation, 166, 167, 204
    WebHelp, 166, 167, 204
Bulleted lists
    creating, 46
    sorting, 46, 196
Chinese
    unofficial support for, 28
CHM files
    building, 166, 167, 204
    publishing, 168, 204
Code Editor, 23
Concept links
    creating, 88
Condition tags
    applying to a folder, 154, 203
    applying to a TOC, 203
    applying to a TOC book or page, 156, 203
    applying to a topic or file, 154, 203
    applying to an index entry, 157
    applying to content, 155
    applying to topics, 155

    importing, 152
Content folder, 27, 194
Context-sensitive help
    alias files, 173, 205
    header files, 171
    testing, 175, 205
CSS files
    creating, 122, 201
Danish
    support for, 27
Dictionary
    converting from RoboHelp, 33
DOC files
    creating projects based on, 57
    importing, 60, 195
Document dock, 99
DotNet Help, 11, 15, 159, 191
    building, 166, 167, 204
    publishing, 168, 204
    viewing, 167, 204
Dutch
    support for, 27
Fantastischen, 4
Finnish
    support for, 27
Flare
    clean code, 11
    XML-based architecture, 11
FlashHelp, 17, 160
flprj files, 28, 57
Folders
    applying condition tags, 154, 203
Footer proxy, 133
FPJ files
    why Flare doesn't use them, 192
FrameMaker
    announced support for, 19
French
    support for, 27
German
    support for, 27
Germany, 4
    Brazil, 0

Glossary
    adding terms, 115
    associating with a target, 118
    creating, 113, 200
    enabling in a skin, 118
    in HTML Help, 119
Glossary links
    inserting, 117
Glossary proxy, 133
GUI
    compared to RoboHelp, 25
    emulating RoboHelp, 99, 114
Header (.h) files, 171
Header proxy, 133
HMTL Help
    viewing, 167, 204
HTML files
    importing, 24
HTML Help
    browse sequences, 97
    building, 166, 167, 204
    publishing, 168, 204
Importing
    HTML files, 24
    RoboHelp projects, 30, 194
Index
    auto-creating, 22
    creating, 22
    Index Entry mode, 110
    Index Entry window, 108
    proxy, 133
    showing or hiding markers, 110
    viewing in help systems, 111
Italian
    support for, 27
Japanese
    unofficial support for, 28
JavaHelp
    lack of support for, 17
Kadov tags, 35
Keyword links
    creating, 87
Links, 69, 73, 197
    creating concept links, 88
    creating jumps, 69
    creating keyword links, 87
    creating related topics links, 86
    creating text popups, 77
    creating topic popups, 75
Lists, 45
    creating, 46

sorting, 46, 196
Master pages
    associating with a target, 134
    creating, 23, 132
    inserting proxies, 133
mchelp file
    building, 166, 167, 204
    publishing, 168, 204
Microsoft Word
    support for, 13
Mini-toc proxy, 133
Norwegian
    support for, 27
Numbered lists
    creating, 46
Oracle Help
    lack of support for, 18
Output folder, 27, 33, 159, 192, 194, 204, 205
Page footer proxy, 133
Page header proxy, 133
PDF files
    announced support for, 19
Popups
    creating text popups, 77
    creating topic popups, 75
Portuguese
    support for, 27
Portuguese (Brazilian)
    support for, 27
Printed documentation
    building, 166, 167, 204
    publishing, 168, 204
    viewing, 167, 204
Project folder, 27, 194
Projects
    creating, 28, 57
    importing RoboHelp projects, 30, 194
Proxies
    breadcrumbs, 133
    glossary, 133
    index, 133
    inserting into a master page, 133
    mini-toc, 133
    page footer, 133
    page header, 133
    TOC, 133
    topic body, 133

Publishing
    destinations, 168, 204
    DotNet Help, 168, 204
    HTML Help, 168, 204
    printed documentation, 168, 204
    WebHelp, 168, 204
Related topics links
    creating, 86
RoboHelp
    compared to Flare, 23
    emulating its interface, 99, 114
    how Flare converts files, 192
    importing into Flare, 30, 194
    WebHelp comparison, 160
RoboHelp conversion
    custom dictionary, 33, 34
    index file, 107
    templates, 131
Russian
    unofficial support for, 28
Section 508, 66, 71, 72, 74, 76
    support for, 13, 23
Skins, 34, 135, 191
    associating with a target, 138
    converting from RoboHelp, 34
    creating, 135, 201
    editing, 137
    enabling a browse sequence, 96
    enabling a glossary, 118
    importing, 136
Snippets, 145, 146, 191
Span bar, 42
Spanish
    support for, 27
Structure bars, 42
Style mediums
    creating, 127
Styles
    creating, 122, 124, 127, 201
    modifying, 125
Stylesheets, 121, 127, 192
    associating with topics, 128
    creating, 122, 201
    importing, 123
    table stylesheets, 12, 16, 50
Swedish
    suport for, 27
Table stylesheets, 12, 16, 50
Tables, 47
    applying table stylesheets, 12, 16, 50
    creating, 47, 196
    table row and column bars, 42
Tag bar, 42
Targets, 33, 159, 192, 204, 205
    associating a skin, 138
    building, 166, 167, 204
    creating, 162, 204
    publishing, 168, 204
    selecting a browse sequence, 96
    selecting a glossary, 118
    selecting a master page, 134
Templates
    converting RoboHelp, 131
    using, 22
Text Editor, 40
Text popups
    creating, 77
TOCs
    applying condition tags, 156, 203
    associating with a target, 106
    auto-generating, 22, 102
    creating, 100
    creating multiple, 104
    docking, 99
    linking, 105
    proxy, 133
Topic body proxy, 133
Topic popups
    creating, 75
Topic titles
    finding, 39
Topics
    applying condition tags, 154, 155, 157, 203
    associating with a stylesheet, 128
    closing all, 43
    creating, 37, 195, 197
    finding an open topic, 43
    opening, 40, 41
    opening in the code editor, 23, 40
    opening multiple, 11, 21
    opening two topics side by side, 41
    structure bars, 42
UI
    compared to RoboHelp, 25

emulating RoboHelp, 99, 114
Undo
　multiple, 11
Variable sets
　creating, 140
Variables, 12, 16, 139, 164, 165, 202
　system, 12, 139, 144
WCAG, 66, 71, 72, 74, 76
WebHelp
　building, 166, 167, 204
　Flare vs RoboHelp, 23, 160
　viewing, 167, 204
Word
　support for, 13
Word documents
　creating projects based on, 57
XHTML, 37
XML, 37
XML Editor, 40, 41

MadCap's support forums

Check out MadCap Software's online knowledge base and peer-to-peer forums for the latest information about Flare. Just go to **www.madcapsoftware.com**.

Flare training

User First Services offers certified Flare training and consulting. You can also sign-up for our Flare Tips and Tricks email newsletter. For more information, visit our website at **www.userfirst.net**.